A
Lancaster Pilot's
Impression
on Germany

By

Richard (Dick) Starkey
Ex Flt/Lt

Published in the United Kingdom by Compaid Graphics
5 St. Peter Street, Blackburn. Lancashire. BB2 2HD

ISBN 1 900604 09 4

First Edition February 1999
Reprinted 2004

Dedication

My wonderful wife, Jean who passed away in 2002.

Acknowledgments

Two friends who deserve a special mention are Jonathan and Jean who encouraged me to write my story and made all the arrangements for the visits to Germany in 1997 and 1998.

Jonathan drove over 800 miles so that I could visit the sites and buildings where I was held in captivity at places hundreds of miles apart i.e. Oberhausel, Konigsberg, Meiningen, Obermassfeld.

Also the War Graves Cemetery at Hanover and The Armament Museum at Koblenz.

The others who deserve a mention are :-

Mrs Janet Cross who typed the text.

The Lepper family(Irwin, Lina, Dr Herman and Sylvia)

Herbert Griebel, Virma and Lina Reinhardt

(All of Konigsberg, near Wetzlar, Germany)

Gretel Reeh and staff at the Bergoff/Remuhle, Konigsberg

Wilhelm and Frau Schupp, Konigsberg

Martin West, Rancher, Konigsberg

Martin Becker, German Nightfighter Ace and his Navigator/Radar Operator

Staff at the Wetzlar Information Centre

Doncaster Air Gunners Association

Martin Middlebrook, Author. *The Nuremberg Raid*

Sgt Williams, Parachute Section, RAF Coningsby

Mr Cowley, Irvins Parachute (Great Britain)

Panton Bros and Staff, East Kirby Air Museum

Gary Francis, Photographer, Gawber, Barnsley

Eric Millett, artist, Anglesey

Mike Mansfield, Compaid Graphics, Warrington

Peter Hincliffe. O.B.E. M.I.L.

Sunday Telegraph.

Contents

Introduction

When you reach the twilight of your life and you want to write a story about a part of it you should do so as soon as possible before memories cloud over and fade away.

So I am writing my story before the sun sets.

It is now part of History and covers a five year period in the Second World War which was over fifty years ago, but as I write it all seems to have happened yesterday as one story leads to another.

I have a small plastic box in front of me containing part of a red switch from Lancaster 'Q' Queenie, the aircraft I flew on many operations with No. 106 Squadron 5 Group Bomber Command stationed at Metheringham, Lincolnshire in 1943 / 1944.

A friend of mine Jonathan Wroe who persuaded me to write the story identified it as part of the 'G' set which was a Navigational Aid. We found it in June 1997 at the site where the Lancaster crashed after I was shot down near the village of Konigsberg, Central Germany in March 1944 and from where we started a journey to retrace my steps in captivity, but more of that later.

As for the title of the book it seemed appropriate after my impact on German soil.

Chapter 1

Air Crew Receiving Centre and Initial Training Wing

I was eighteen years of age when I volunteered for air crew duties, Royal Air Force in April 1941.

I had a medical examination locally the same as everybody else who was joining the forces, and was then sent to R.A.F. Cardington for air crew medical and aptitude tests for three days before returning home on deferred service to await recall as an R.A.F. flying cadet. Four months later in August 1941 I received orders to report to Air Crew Receiving Centre (A.C.R.C.) at Lords Cricket Ground London where I joined several hundred more on the same intake. All meals at the Air Crew Receiving Centre were taken in one of the cafeterias in Regents Park Zoo, and as we were billeted in flats opposite the park, were awakened every morning by all kinds of strange animal noises, mostly monkeys ; it all seemed a far cry from the noise made by domestic pets. It was at the Reception Centre in London that I made friends with another Cadet from Preston. His Father lived in the City, I think it was Bayswater, where he had a flat.

After we had been there a few days my friend told me his Dad had invited him over and to bring a friend.

When we arrived there we were greeted by his Father who introduced us to his friends both male and female.

Now around August 1941 a film presentation of 'The Mikado' in colour was being shown around the country with very good notices. At that time Gilbert and Sullivan operettas were very popular and The Mikado was top of the list.

A singer from the U.S.A. called Kenny Baker was the leading male singer and the main female singer called Jean Collins was an English girl ; both of them were well known on both sides of the Atlantic. My friends' Father must have had some connection with show business because during the evening a young lady with a very good voice sang to the Company.

We were introduced to her and who should it be but Miss Collins ; now for a lad of eighteen this was quite an occasion meeting a film star.

I had my first taste of whisky that night and I thought my throat had caught fire.

Nevertheless it was a memorable night but my friend and I departed to different I.T.W.'s at the end of a fortnight.

During the next fortnight we were given various tests including night vision to determine whether we were suitable to train as pilots ; I passed the test and was then posted in a party of seventy cadets to an Initial Training Wing (I.T.W.) Torquay to learn about Navigation, Airmanship and Morse Code etc. we were also trained to march in

2

Self and Nick in Flying kit at ITW 1941

various formations, from slow to 120 steps per minute, which was the rate at which we marched to lectures in various buildings around the town.

We also participated in active sports durin two afternoons a week when we played Football, Golf or Swimming which together with several runs of two to three miles per week brought us up to a good physical shape.

We had little time for social activities but I recall Christmas Eve 1941 when a group of cadets were invited to a party given by some young ladies from the Prudential Insurance Company who had been evacuated from London to Torquay and were living in a small hotel near Daddy Hole Plain. It was quite a night amongst some very beautiful girls who made sure everyone joined in the night's activities. When the 'Conga' was called we flummoxed the lady who kept an eye on the girls. The 'line' was moving slowly in the room when it was diverted through the door and into the blackout on Daddy Hole Plain where someone shouted 'every man for himself' and as all the cadets and girls knew every corner of that piece of Torquay the 'Conga' disintegrated ; every one disappearing into the night.

When they reappeared at the party the festive mood really took hold with the lady in charge putting a guard on the door.

After six weeks at I.T.W. we took an examination on all the subjects studied during the course, of which Navigation was the most challenging as it included Algebra Maths and Trigonometry.

If a cadet passed the examination he was promoted to a rank of Leading Aircraftsman and was ready to start his flying training.

In January 1942 I was posted to an E.F.T.S. (Elementary Flying Training School) at Desford near Leicester and commenced flying training on Tiger Moths.

The weather was atrocious as snow lay on the ground. Visibility was poor and we were instructed to fly straight and level by using the nose of the aircraft in relation to the horizon but as there was no horizon it was always very misty, we could not see it and found it difficult to fly straight and level.

We were supposed to be graded as to our adaptability to fly before joining the Empire Air Training Scheme to commence our real training. I flew 6 hours dual instruction at Desford and only hoped the weather would be better when I started my flying training overseas.

From Desford I was sent to Heaton Park Reception Centre, Manchester where air crew cadets were assembled before transferring to Canada, Rhodesia or U.S.A. where the weather was always favourable for flying, I was put on reserve for a party going to Rhodesia, and as it was very rare for someone on reserve to be called on, I was sure I would probably be going to Canada with the next party.

However when the party for Rhodesia was assembled one of the cadets was missing; after several minutes trying to locate him, without success, I was detailed to take his place, but as I joined the parade to proceed to the railway station the missing cadet appeared. I was relieved because I wanted to train in Canada or the U.S.A.

Initial Training Wing intake 1941

Self - second from left front row

Chapter 2

U.S.A. and Canada

The next day my name was included in a party sailing to the States where we would travel by train to a Reception Centre at Monkton, New Brunswick Canada. From there we would either go west to Manitoba Saskatchewan, Alberta or south to the U.S.A. (Alabama or Florida).

We sailed from Gourock, Scotland in February 1942 in a converted banana boat named U.S.S. Neville, eleven thousand tons, and for the first two days were escorted by corvettes of the Royal Navy. This was the time when U-boats hunted in wolf packs and they had sunk hundreds of thousands of tons of Allied shipping so far that year.

After two days we saw smoke on the horizon and as we approached the Area saw many Warships which were part of the U.S. Atlantic Fleet. America had been in the War for two months after the bombing of Pearl Harbour and from what we saw they had plenty of ships in the Atlantic for convoy protection.

I was in the second hold below deck along with many more cadets. We were battened down every night which made us feel abandoned ; if anything happened we should be left to our fate.

It did not help our morale when depth charges were dropped during the hours of darkness and everyone kept their fingers crossed and said a silent prayer for their survival. At night time the U-boats gathered in wolf packs and attacked convoys, some of them at times surfaced and got among the convoy undetected in the darkness.

We were told after one night of heavy depth charging that a U-boat had been sunk.

As the convoy approached the American Coast we were met by a Dirigible, which gave us overhead protection. It was a kind of airship used by the Americans to spot U-boats. Everyone was getting excited and when we finally saw the coast a great cheer went up.

The boat sailed up the Hudson River passing the Statue of Liberty which was a symbol of freedom and protection especially to European Immigrants who had been able to flee Nazi Germany after Hitler came to power, some of them had been persecuted and although we did not know it at the time, thousands more were locked away in concentration camps.

I remember one chap in our party who came from Accrington ; on seeing the Statue of Liberty for the first time said in a broad Lancashire accent "It's just like Blackpool Tower".

We disembarked at New York and as we came off the boat saw something that will never be seen again. The three largest liners in the world at that time namely, Queen Mary, Queen Elizabeth and the

Normandie, the French vessel, all over eighty thousand tons, berthed side by side. Because of their size the two Queens had commenced transporting troops across the Atlantic and also sailed into the southern Hemisphere both unescorted because they had the speed to evade U-boats. The Normandie was lying on its side after fire had recently damaged it and took no further part in the War.

We disembarked onto a train which was standing next to the ship, and for the next few hours made ourselves familiar with the accommodation. We would be travelling overnight and would pass through the New England countryside. It was all very exciting after the days of tension on the North Atlantic crossing.

The train pulled out of the docks at around midnight and the first part of the journey took us through the outskirts of New York, where for the first time in two and a half years we saw street lights.

Everyone settled down to an uninterrupted sleep which was a welcome relief after the recent sleepless nights on the boat. We awoke as the train passed through New England with its beautiful countryside, made even more so by the blossoming trees and the white painted quaint wooden buildings.

The train stopped at Bangor Main where the citizens of that city entertained us at the station. They had a great respect for the R.A.F. and now that their Army Airforce would soon be joining the air attack on Germany hoped that they would be as good if not better than the Luftwaffe crews.

We arrived at Monkton in the evening and were marched to a huge Camp on the outskirts of the town which was both a receiving and distribution centre for all training schools in Canada and the U.S.A., and also a holding station for trained air crew returning to England.

After two days we left Monkton and started a five day rail journey across Canada to an E.F.T.S. at Moose Jaw Saskatchewan travelling first on Canadian National Railway for one and a half days and the remainder of the trip on Canadian Pacific Railway, a journey which made you realise the immense size of the Country.

The memories of travelling all that time on a train are still embedded in my mind.

The first stop was Montreal where we arrived after thirty six hours, and transferred to a Canadian Pacific Railway train, which would be our home for the next three and a half days.

The following afternoon there was a four hour stop at Ottawa, the Canadian capital, where we had sight of a spectacle that occurs every year in the spring, the breaking up of ice on the mighty St. Lawrence river opening up the waterway after the winter freeze up.

There were blocks of ice as big as football fields floating by as we watched from under the towers of the Parliament Building.

On returning to the train we knew we had three days travelling before we reached Moose Jaw but there was still a magnificent view of the

7

Great Lakes to look forward to. On the fourth day we were on the prairies, the journey taking us through the massive corn belt. During the morning we arrived at Winnipeg where a pleasant surprise awaited us ; a reception by the Local Air Force Society who provided refreshments, a welcome to Canada, and music and dancing before we again boarded the train.

After five days of travelling from New Brunswick we arrived at Caron near Moose Jaw. It was a 'whistle stop station' with wheat storage towers, common to the prairies and a few houses with probably one hundred residents.

There was nothing else in view, apart from the R.A.F. Camp two miles away, it was the prairie from horizon to horizon with a line of small foothills in the distance. A dirt road led to the Camp which as described was in the middle of nowhere.

The station personnel were housed in 'H' blocks with ground and upstairs floors and ablutions connecting the dormitories on either side.

Paddy Moroney from Southern Ireland. E.F.T.S. Moose Jaw, Sask, Canada.

An Elementary Flying Training course on Tiger Moths usually lasted eight weeks which was taken up with lectures and flying. The course was split into two flights, one flying in the morning, with lectures in the afternoon and vice versa for the other flight.

Because of severe turbulence over the prairies in late May and June due to the hot weather, flying a Tiger Moth could be very bumpy so during that period flying training was undertaken in two periods ; the first commencing at

8

6am and finishing at twelve noon, and the afternoon class flew between 2pm and 8pm.

Sixty hours dual and solo had to be flown to complete the course, and pupils usually made their first solo flight after five to seven hours dual with an instructor, mostly circuits and bumps, then you went on to aerobatics cross country flights, and finally a few hours night flying.

During the summer when it was dry, dust storms were common on the prairies and eye shields were worn for protection. These storms suddenly sprang up as strong winds took hold and made flying very difficult, especially landing.

I remember one flight with an Instructor when the wind suddenly increased as we took off ; it appeared we were not going anywhere and on looking over the side of the cockpit the airfield was still underneath us.

The Instructor aborted the flight and as he turned the aircraft onto the circuit for landing, the tail wind sped us so quickly that he had to turn the aircraft into wind to descend with almost full throttle and nose down. It was difficult to land because on touching down the wind could have turned us over, but we managed to taxi to dispersal where the aircraft was tied down.

Although night flying was restricted to a few hours at Caron, some hair raising incidents occurred, and on one or two occasions pupils mistook the dimly lit streets of Caron two miles down the road for the flare-path which was lit with gooseneck flares, and had made landing approaches nearly to touchdown before realising their mistakes.

There was also an American Instructor who came from Texas, and he was known to try and herd cattle together with his Tiger Moth when flying low over the ranches.

Sometimes you became nostalgic especially at night when in the barracks you could see the lights of the Trans Canadian Express as it thundered through the prairies on the railway line which ran two miles away through Caron, and as it approached the crossing in the village it used its wailing whistle which was a familiar sound on films. I do not know why but it made one think of home.

I remember one non flying incident and it related to a China man who had a cafe, called Smokey Joes opposite the Camp gates, it was just a shack with nothing behind it but the prairie.

One day I was waiting for the Camp bus which ran from Moose Jaw to Caron when a Royal Canadian Mounted police car pulled up and asked me if I wanted a lift to Camp. After getting into the car and talking in general about the area, they asked me about the China man, I did not know what they were getting at until drugs were mentioned. Naturally I could not give them any information but shortly after Smokey Joes was shut down and the China man was never seen again.

At the end of the course we were given three days leave and together with two other cadets I went to Regina, capital of Saskatchewan where we stayed with a family.

Whilst we were there two famous Hollywood film stars, Walter Pigeon and Susan Haywood stopped at the City to promote the sale of War Bonds and at the time it was something to remember because in England the only time you saw a Hollywood star was on the screen (there were no televisions) and Susan had the most beautiful natural red hair, she took part in several epics made in that era.

I completed my sixty hours flying training at the end of June and after passing the Chief flying Instructors test was ready for the next stage which was service flying training school. The school chosen for the course was at Calgary in Alberta and we left Caron at the beginning of July to travel overnight by train to that City. We arrived on Sunday morning and much to our surprise were told the famous Calgary Stampede opened on the Monday.

Calgary is about a hundred miles or less from the Canadian Rockies which at the time we arrived I was told could be seen very clearly. I looked to the west but could not see them when everyone else could, I thought this very strange until my eyes focused and to my surprise instead of being a low line on the horizon, which I expected, their snow capped peaks were towering over us as though they were five miles away.

The airfield was situated on a plateau about two miles from the City and was owned by the Civil Aviation Authorities, but one side of the field was taken over by the R.A.F. to train pilots on Airspeed Oxford, a single wing two engined aircraft which was the main aircraft for training multi-engined pilots in England.

The aircraft at Calgary had been transferred from the U.K. during the previous two years and many pilots had already trained on them. They were getting a bit ancient and as the airfield was 4,000 feet above sea level it was difficult to maintain height when practising single-engined flying.

The Oxford was also recognised as a difficult aircraft to fly with one or two nasty characteristics, which made the pilot extra careful. For instance it had a vicious stall and would drop either wing without warning (shuddering) during that manoeuvre so the pilot had to be fully alert.

It was said an Oxford never flew the same way on consecutive approaches before landing and the pilot had to fly it all the time and not let the aircraft fly him.

There was also another training aircraft on Service Flying Training, the Avro Anson which had no vices at all and was so easy to fly it was said it could land itself.

This was the aircraft everyone wanted to fly at S.F.T.S. because the pass rate was higher ; however when we had flown the Oxford successfully and passed our wings test we all felt very confident about flying the larger multi-engined aircraft. At this point I will again refer to the Calgary Stampede as it took place during our first week when we were given two days off to watch the opening procession and some of the riding, roping and chuck wagon racing.

The procession was very colourful with the Red Indians all dressed in their ceremonial gear and cowgirls and cowboys riding their magnificent horses. There were also a number of Royal Canadian Mounted Police in colourful tunics riding their horses. The star of the week was a trick riding cowboy named Monty Montana from Hollywood. He was also a stand in for some of the cowboy stars in films when a scene required some dangerous riding, he could do almost anything whilst riding horses including shooting and roping.

The Stadium where all the events took place in Calgary included a full Red Indian Camp site with all the colour seen on the films. There were some exciting events including Bronco busting, Steer roping and Chuck Wagon racing ; the latter very dangerous as the men drove a team of four horses pulling a small covered wagon racing round a circuit, never reducing speed, with the inevitable ending when some of the wagons overturned. It was a wonder that only a few riders and horses were injured.

After eight hours instruction on the Oxford, I flew solo ; the aircraft by comparison to the Tiger Moth was heavy on the controls.

At the Service Flying Training School one instructor normally had three cadets to teach, and the one our trio had was given to rages, tearing his helmet off and telling us in no uncertain manner what he thought of some of our efforts. We were all treated the same way, and often discussed his attitude which never changed.

However, one day I was talking to one of the other cadets and asked him how he was getting on with the Instructor.

He said their relationship was great because he had stopped calling him a
" c..t " and now called him a "bloody clot".

There was a satellite airfield in open country about ten miles from the main aerodrome and we used to fly over there to practice circuits and bumps and single-engined flying and landings.

The course became very interesting when we started cross country flights when one cadet flew the plane and another navigated ; the next day the roles were reversed. Navigating was very easy because roads ran east and west and north and south even though there were few of them. The best guide if anyone happened to get lost was the Canadian Pacific Railway which ran east and west, so one had only to follow the lines. However there was no need to cheat because navigation was easy. Lake Louise was within easy reach of the airfield and the Instructor would fly over it frequently. However a Hollywood Studio decided to make a film on location there, so for a few weeks it was out of flying bounds. The reason the film was made at Lake Louise was the beautiful scenery which did justice to the production. It was called 'Springtime in the Rockies' with Betty Grable, a Wartime glamour film star and a favourite of both the American and British forces. After the War it was shown many times on T.V.

One of the hazards of flying from Calgary in summer were forest fires in the Rockies, when the wind came from the west which was frequent. The smoke from them made visibility very hazy up to three thousand feet, and in the evening as the sun dropped in the west flying became dangerous because many planes were in the air around the airfield, waiting to land. A pilot had to be fully alert, especially if he was flying solo. Fortunately there were no accidents whilst I was there.

At the end of September 1942 Flying Training Command decided to swap stations with the Havards, a single-engined advanced trainer at Swift Current in Saskatchewan. This was because the Oxfords were becoming unsuitable for single-engined flying at 4,000 feet, and as the airfield at Swift Current was at a lower altitude than Calgary it would be better to move the Training School there.

Swift Current is situated between Moose Jaw and Calgary and it took about two and a half hours to fly there (I have still got the maps showing our track). At that time it had not got the entertainment (cinemas etc.) like Calgary, but as our course would finish in about four weeks all we wanted to do was get on with the flying and receive our pilots wings.

Shortly after arriving at Swift Current I was devastated when I received news my Mother had passed away. It was a shock because a telephone message was received at the station notifying me of her passing before I received a cable from my Dad in England saying she was seriously ill.

I was numbed because although she had been ill for some time I did not expect to receive the news of her death, especially before the cable arrived.

I was so shocked that I was taken off flying for the day.

Training continued as did the classroom lectures because it was getting near the time for the Wings Exam which was held over three days, and a lot of swotting had to be done at night. For instance the Navigation Exam lasted for three hours and the examiners used a Navigation Log from an actual operation over Germany to set the problems for the Flight Plan and the full Navigation chart we had to compile.

One hundred and fifty hours had to be flown during Service Flying Training and in the latter part of the course a lot of those hours were taken up by cross countries day and night. The night cross countries were flown solo and although they were short it was a bit nerve racking being 'up there' on your own in darkness. You made sure you flew smack on compass course, and there were also the dim lights of the small prairie hamlets to give you 'pin points'.

Going back to the two people in the Oxford on cross country exercises, i.e. one piloting and one navigating, I sometimes flew with a pal of mine.

12

George Rowley (Co pilot & navigator cross countries). S.F.T. School, Swift Current, Sask, Canada

He had volunteered for aircrew when he was twenty five years of age and had just an ordinary elementary education so he was not familiar with geometry and trigonometry, two of the subjects required when navigating.

Before exams I used to help him with his maths and he managed to obtain the necessary marks.

However when he was navigating in the air he had difficulty with maintaining his calculations due to the many points which required constant attention, i.e. recognising land marks with consequent alterations of course due to the finding of a new wind speed and direction.

When I was flying the aircraft and the time came to alter course he would stand behind me, tap me on the shoulder and with a straight arm indicated which way I should turn, left or right. Now visibility in Saskatchewan in summer is almost unlimited and on this particular occasion we were flying from Swift Current to Regina so as the latter stood out like a sore thumb on the prairies, even though we were many miles away, as soon as the nose of the aircraft came in line with our destination he would point straight ahead.

I often think about these exercises and the way he carried them out ; it was very funny to see him indicating the turn and then pointing straight ahead as if giving instructions to a car driver.

When we returned to Base I would help him to back track his log and chart by using the amended headings and calculated wind speeds before handing both to the Navigation Instructor, who I am sure had an idea of our fixing ' the log' but let it pass.

There were three Chief Flying Instructor's tests during the course, one when you were ready to fly the Oxford solo, another after fifty hours, and the third and final one, the Wings Test at about a hundred and forty five hours. During the latter one a cadet had to satisfy the Chief Flying Instructor that he was a competent pilot and ready for his Pilots Wings.

If I remember rightly statistics indicated that in an intake of seventy aircrew cadet pilots, twenty five would finally receive their Pilots Wings and the remainder would re-muster to other aircrew duties, i.e. Navigators, Wireless Operators, Air Gunners, Bomb Aimers and Engineers.

When I completed the Wings Test I had about four hours flying to complete the programme. It was the beginning of November and temperatures had fallen considerably as the Canadian winter approached.

The change happened overnight when ice formed and snow fell, conditions which would remain the same until the following spring. The snow was rolled and left on the airfield, and starting the engines in such weather was a slow and very cold job for the ground crews.

I remember my last flight to complete the four hours required. It was a very cold but sunny day, and it was clear so I decided to fly a cross country to fill the time.

Montana State in the USA is south of Saskatchewan and as Swift Current was not far off the border I decided to fly west following the Canadian Pacific Railway for a timed run before turning south to fly a few miles into Montana and then turn back and return to base.

I completed the first part of the flight to a point west of Swift Current by flying along the Canadian Pacific Railway then turned south towards Montana. The weather was still good and visibility clear so I continued south into the State over desolate country but could not see any sign of habitation. I felt quite lonely but as I still had two hours of flying to complete my training, decided to fly around and look for anything interesting on the ground.

I had not noticed the weather was deteriorating from the west ; so I turned north on the return journey when I saw storm clouds approaching from the west. I was a long way from the airfield and decided it would be quicker to turn north east in order to hit the railway line nearer Swift Current and keep my eye on the storm. When I reached the railway line about ten miles from base it was about five miles away.

I turned east and soon saw the Camp where aircraft were queuing up to land ; I joined the circuit and just as I made a landing, the storm which was actually a blizzard, hit the airfield and snow reduced visibility to about twenty yards. Not only that but as I taxied to dispersal the port engine stopped and I had to abandon the aircraft.

I realised afterwards that if I hadn't noticed the storm approaching, I would have been caught in it over unfriendly terrain with only one good engine which could have been disastrous if it had stopped.

So my last flight in Canada was a memorable one.

The 'Wings Parade' took place two days after followed by an end of course dinner at an hotel in Swift Current ; I still have the menu and signatures of some of the pilots both Instructors and pupils.

14

At the end of Service Flying Training and before returning to England many of the trainees wanted to realise a lifetime ambition and visit Hollywood. At the end of most courses leave was granted and a lot of us had saved up enough money to go to the Film City.

Everyone's ambition was to see Deanna Durbin who at the time was the favourite young film star of the Royal Air Force Cadets, she sang beautifully and some of her songs are still available.

Three instructors had spent a leave in Hollywood and were fortunate to meet her whilst she was making a film. They gave a detailed report in the Station Magazine of their meeting with her, which had been arranged for them by Nigel Bruce a British actor who for many years played Doctor Watson with Basil Rathbone's Sherlock Holmes in the films of that title.

Nigel Bruce was the actor to contact when you arrived there and he was good enough to make arrangements for Cadets to have an enjoyable leave. However our course did not receive any leave and the day after we received our wings were on the train for the long journey east to Monkton.

We stayed at Monkton for a week and then boarded a train for New York to embark for the U.K. to complete further training before joining a squadron.

The Queen Elizabeth was waiting at New York and as soon as the train stopped we were transferred to the big liner which had been completed earlier in the War and fitted for troop accommodation.

The cabins on either side of the corridors where we were berthed had to be used on a shift basis i.e. nights, days and afternoons. This was due to a massive troop movement of twenty eight thousand of which 95% were Americans. Each individual was given a ticket to feed twice every twenty four hours at some of the oddest times, i.e. 3.00 o'clock in the afternoon and 3.00am in the morning but everyone could take away extra food from the mess to carry them over until the next meal time.

Metal beds were also fitted on the walls of the Promenade Deck which was blacked out by shuttering every night.

The Boat was to travel across the Atlantic at high speed unescorted which we hoped would be too fast for the U-boats to get within torpedo range, it was also assumed it would take more than one torpedo to sink her.

We sailed out of the Hudson River on a Tuesday morning in November and by next morning must have travelled South because the temperature was high and the weather was perfect. After that however as the Ship zig-zagged east across the Atlantic the weather turned colder and unsettled and everyone's eyes were on the look out for U-boats. On standing at the stern and looking back at the zig-zagging course and the speed at which we were travelling it made one's mind easier about arriving safely.

15

Arrive, we did at Gourock, Scotland on Sunday midday having taken five days for the crossing which had been anything but direct.

When the Ship docked, all the Americans disembarked but all British aircrew were left to guard the ship for two days until the next contingent for sailing came aboard. During that time we were allowed all over the Ship and as it was the largest in the World at that time, some of the rooms, e.g. dining, ballroom were enormous ; we were very impressed.

Chapter 3

Return to United Kingdom flying refresher courses

On leaving the ship aircrew personnel were put on a train to travel to Harrogate which was a Holding Centre for Commonwealth Trained Airmen. The Commonwealth Air Training Scheme was in full swing by the end of 1942, and because of the large number of aircrew coming through, a bottle neck had materialised which delayed the dispersal of men to flying duties, so Harrogate became a Holding Centre.

On arrival at Harrogate most of the party were taken to the Majestic Hotel which had been taken over by the R.A.F., but I was included in a party that was billeted at the Grand Hotel, much smaller than the Majestic.

We spent our time doing route marches and having lectures but were soon on our way to Whitley Bay for an R.A.F. Regiment Course where we were put into semi-detached houses which the owners had left to accommodate R.A.F. airmen.

It was February 1943 by this time and we had not flown an aircraft since leaving Canada in November, so the pilots at Whitley Bay were getting 'browned off'. It was a fact that trained aircrew were returning from the Commonwealth but were not being posted to operational training. However later in the year and the early part of 1944 would see things change when Bomber Command would suffer hundreds of casualties.

In March after returning to Harrogate I was posted to Perth, Scotland for a month on what was to be a worthwhile course of flying.

The airfield was at Scone and we flew Tiger Moths with a Navigator who had trained overseas, and like the pilots were waiting for further training.

Generally we flew over local flying areas, but we also flew cross country routes.

I remember one of these vividly, we were to fly south to Montrose then inland before returning north to Perth. As we approached our first turning point at Montrose a Spitfire came from that direction, and the pilot waved his arms ; we thought he was being friendly to the occupants of a Tiger Moth and waved back.

The Spitfire naturally soon passed by because of his superior speed, but then turned back towards us and flew near stalling speed with wheels and flaps down. Again he waved, even more frantically, and again we waved back, whereupon he flew to us as near as possible and formed the words

" get down".

By this time I knew he was serious and put the nose of the plane down descending to one hundred feet and looked for the railway line that would take us back to Perth.

It gave me the chance to do a bit of low flying, but we were puzzled as to the reason for the Spitfire pilot's action.

We found out when we arrived back at the airfield and reported the incident. Evidently German aircraft were raiding shipping in the Firth of Forth just south of our position and Spitfires had shot down two of them.

Apart from this incident it was like flying in peace time ; we could plan our cross country routes and fly to interesting places in the area.

On one cross country we flew to Dyce Airfield near Aberdeen, the weather was a bit misty and identifying pin points on the ground was a bit difficult. We flew on our Flight Plan E.T.A. and as we neared the destination I saw a stretch of water on the starboard side in the hazy sunlight. I told the Navigator it was a lake but on looking through the mist saw it was bigger than a lake and realised I had mistakenly identified the North Sea.

There was one other incident when we were flying locally and saw a Tiger Moth overturned with its yellow belly showing and the pilot frantically waving his arms to attract our attention. It was from Scone so I flew round him at low level and made signs that we were returning to base.

We reported the aircraft's whereabouts when we arrived back, and the pilot was brought back by road, but the aircraft was dismantled and brought back by carrier.

The pilot had evidently tried to make a forced landing when his engine cut out, not knowing how boggy the field was and as soon as he touched down the aircraft overturned.

He was shaken but not injured.

I returned to Harrogate at the end of March with some satisfaction, having a few more flying hours albeit on Tiger Moths but looking forward to the next stage.

This was a refresher course on the good old Oxford at Weston-on-the Green near Oxford. It was very similar to the S.F.T.S. programme and lasted two months, part of the course was taken up by a Beam Approach Course at Grantham which lasted a week.

At this point I have to say that an R.A.F. Bomber Pilot in the Second World War had to attain a very high standard of instrument flying and many hours were spent training on aircraft and the Link Trainer to reach this standard. The course at Grantham certainly helped me, every flight was with an instructor and flown under a canopy, so everything depended on correct reading of the instruments ; on take offs, cross country flights and landing by Beam Approach Standard.

Land marks were pin pointed during cross country flights, when for a minute or two you emerged from under the canopy and if you remembered the headings flown, it enabled you to identify the landmark, usually a town or a lake.

18

There is one particular story, nothing to do with flying, and it happened whilst I was travelling on leave from Weston-on-the-Green. I travelled from Oxford to Peterborough and changed trains, having some time to spare I decided to visit the Cathedral. However when I arrived there quite a lot of people, mostly female, were surrounding a very tall American Air Force Officer outside the building. It was Clark Gable, a famous film star who starred in 'Gone with the Wind' which was released in the U.K. during 1943.

There were some pretty good sporting facilities at Weston-on-the-Green and the Station had an excellent soccer team with nine pre-war professionals.

The Sports Officer was an ex amateur soccer international and although our course was made up of only fourteen pilots, including one Canadian and one Australian, he suggested we form a team to take on one of the Station Section Teams. I and another pilot formed a course team and took on the champion Section Team. We gave them a good game and lost only by 1 - 0. ; both the Australian and Canadian played, and I noticed the former was very fast.

There is a post script to the story.

The Australian was called Dennis Carmody and we were posted to different commands after leaving Weston-on-the-Green.

At the end of the War I was repatriated after fifteen months in Germany as a prisoner of War, and on arrival in England was taken to Bicester R.A.F. Station with many more repatriated aircrew, where I again met Dennis Carmody.

Now, after our football games at Weston-on-the-Green in 1943 a few of us on the course had some cricket practice in the nets there. Dennis who was evidently a keen cricketer said to me one evening that as I was a Yorkshireman I should be able to play cricket and would I go to the nets.

There was also another lad who came from Surrey and he could play cricket.

Carmody bowled first with some spin but when he took up the bat both the other chap and myself knew he was a first class batsman, and when we told him he was useful, much better than us, he only smiled.

Anyhow during the summer when I was at O.T.U. (Operational Training Unit) the Sunday newspapers always gave the results of Saturday cricket matches, usually among Service Teams with county players and good overseas players (sometimes internationals who were based in England).

These matches were played at Lords Cricket ground and the Royal Australian Air Force Team, had a team. One of the Sunday newspapers always named the State from which each player came. Every week I read the name Carmody D.P.K. included in the R.A.A.F. team as captain and after a few weeks, came to the conclusion it was Dennis.

When I met him again at Bicester I mentioned this to him and he with a smile said he played for New South Wales and that his cricket tutor was Stan McCabe, second only to Don Bradman as the best batsman in Australia before the War. He said he didn't think he would play for Australia when the test matches resumed, but another R.A.A.F. pilot who had flown Mosquitoes, like him, was coming to see him at Bicester and he would have a place in the test side.

When the pilot arrived he introduced me to him, it was Keith Miller who would become a legend in Australian Test Cricket.

The Australians played a series of Victory Tests at Lords during the summer of 1945 and Miller hit the biggest six seen on that ground in one of the games ; it has never been beaten and the record stands to this day.

Dennis Carmody never made an Australian touring side in England after the War but he invented the 'Carmody Field' which was an umbrella field setting behind the wicket for fast bowlers and used very successfully by the legendary pair Lindwall and Miller.

In the 1980's I wrote to Richie Benaud the Australian Test Commentator and asked him if he could let me know what had happened to Dennis Carmody. He replied that sadly Dennis had passed away in the 1970's, but had been a very good State cricketer and a nice bloke.

Chapter 4

Operational Training Unit

In May 1943 I commenced operational training, and was posted to No.29 Operational Flying Training Unit, North Luffenham.

My first duty was to assemble a crew, and for all aircrew personnel -(Pilot, Navigator, Bomb Aimer, Wireless Operator and Air Gunner), it was an exercise which could have a big influence on their survival. In my case the crew I flew with as Captain and Pilot grew with confidence and reliability through some of the most dangerous operations when Bomber Command suffered heavy losses during the Winter of 1943/44 (including the Battle of Berlin) and I was proud to serve with them.

When crewing up there were no orders on how the make up of each individual team should be made. All aircrew were assembled in one large room and left to their own choices, in my case I did not believe in first impressions, and have never changed my mind on this point, so I was a bit defensive when meeting other aircrew, needing more time to make up my mind ; no doubt as others had with me.

However, everything proceeded without any problems and the outcome for the lads and me turned out satisfactorily.

Here are the names of the crew who came out of the room to fly together as a team :

        Myself   (Captain and Pilot)
        Colin Roberts (Navigator) from Sheffield
        Wally Paris(Bomb Aimer) from East Lothian, Scotland
        George Walker (Wireless Operator) from Northamptonshire
        Joe Ellick (Rear Gunner) from Wallasey

        The other members of the Lancaster Crew e.g. (Flight Engineer and Mid Upper Gunner) would be selected later at Conversion Unit.

We stayed at North Luffenham for a few days and did not fly from that airfield because the Unit was transferred to Bruntingthorpe, South of Leicester in the same month.

As was usual when a unit was moved to another Station everyone was given a task to perform, and our crew were detailed to position ourselves at a T junction in a village two miles from North Luffenham near the Peterborough - Leicester road to direct station traffic onto it. It was only after forty years and whilst visiting my eldest Daughter and her Husband, who had moved to Morcott near Oakham, that I realised their house stood at the same junction.

I often pass North Luffenham Airfield, which is now disused, when I am in Morcott and recognise the aircrew quarters of 1943, and the buildings where Bomber crews teamed up. It is nostalgic but even more poignant and sad when I remember the young men eighteen, nineteen,

Self, Jack, Bob, unknown (Taffy), Colin. 29 O.T.U. Bruntingthorpe

twenty and twenty one years of age who volunteered for aircrew and who I saw there mixing together to form crews who would have an average survival rate of five operations (before they became some of the fifty five thousand casualties in Bomber Command).

We started our Operational Training on Wellingtons at Bitteswell which was the satellite airfield of Bruntingthorpe, at the end of June.

The Wellington was a sturdy aircraft designed by Barnes Wallis, inventor of the bouncing bomb used by No. 617 Squadron on the Ruhr dams.

It was an operational aircraft and flying it was no problem, but it needed some pressure on the control column when landing with flaps down, because the trim was automatic, and you had to watch the airspeed.

There was always some apprehension amongst crews at O.T.U. before the first flight with a pilot ; after all their lives would be in his hands especially on take offs and landings ; and I was told by my crew of remarks made by others, if they had been startled at their pilots handling of the aircraft. They probably didn't appreciate the pilots early flights in the Wellington would be difficult and he had to familiarise himself with the aircraft, some of which had characteristics you didn't expect.

However after flying together for a few days they would all get to know each other ; the pilot would soon be aware of the strength and weakness of each member of his group. It was also very rare for a pilot, at that stage of his service, to be 'washed out'.

We commenced our training with 'Screen' pilots who had completed a tour of operations with Bomber Command and then been posted to O.T.U's.

I flew six hours with these pilots on take offs and landings and overshoots before taking the crew on my own to continue on the exercises.

During part of my Operational Training I had a screen pilot who had a bad stammer. He was a good flyer but found it difficult to give me straightforward instructions. On the few times I flew with him my crew would be at their positions in the aircraft when he came to take the seat next to me.

The first time I waited for him to give me instructions but it took him a long time to get the words out, so when he flew with us again, as soon as he sat in his seat I did not wait for instructions but taxied out along the perimeter track towards the take off point, by which time I thought he would have given me instructions what to do when we were airborne.

These were not always forthcoming and on one occasion I took off, climbed to 1,000ft before he could say "Do a circuit at a 1,000ft.".

I indicated the altimeter already read 1,000ft and he said "O.K. cancel the last instruction", with some difficulty. It was really amusing but he had our sympathy.

The four weeks we spent at Bitteswell covered basic practices required for the crew to operate the aircraft as an efficient team and except for one or two hiccups my crew soon became confident with each other.

We would be doing a lot of night flying during the latter part of the course so it was essential that I could take off and land the aircraft efficiently. Flying over a blacked out country required confident instrument flying, and I made sure the instruments always took precedence over instinct ; flying in darkness sometimes produced disorientation so I always read the instruments to ascertain the position of the aircraft and used them to make any alteration to the aircraft's flying position.

We started night flying cross countries when we returned to Bruntingthorpe, they were called Bull's-eyes ; and during these flights, which took us over several towns we would make reports on the standards of the blackout. I remember one of them, Southport, where the blackout was poor, and Lord street, the main thoroughfare could be identified by the lighting even if it was dim.

It might have been useful to the Luftwaffe when they bombed Liverpool.

We were also liable to be 'attacked' by our own night fighters using radar.

I remember one of these night flights which took us over the east coast between Hull and Scarborough, but we managed to fly nearer Hull and as a consequence became involved with the 'squeakers' an audio warning signal to aircraft when they were nearing barrage balloons which were put up to defend the city. It was a frightening experience made by a loud noise of very high pitch with penetrating shrieks in your ears.

I thought we were smack amongst them, and as the cables on the balloons could cut through the wings of an aircraft, decided to maintain a climbing turn spiralling up to what I thought would be a safe altitude before changing course, I was relieved to get away.

The aircraft had cable cutters on the leading edge to sever cables, but I never knew of any aircraft flying into a Barrage Balloon.

On another night we were on a six hour 'Bull's-eye' which, during summer, covered most of the hours of darkness. Near the end of the flight we were instructed to divert to Upper Heyford in Oxfordshire. When the Navigator gave me a course to fly to the airfield I noticed we were low on fuel having approximately sufficient for thirty minutes flying.

Oxfordshire was covered with airfields and all of them must have been night flying because the drem lights were switched on at all of them, and as the airfields were close together the circles of light overlapped each other.

In order to find an aerodrome during the hours of darkness in Wartime, the first and last letters were illuminated on a different site a few miles from the field each night.

The course from the site, would be known to the crews, so when the letters were identified on any night, the pilot flew the course provided.

We identified the letters for Upper Heyford and I flew the appropriate heading to take us to the field, which was done on a time and distance basis, but when the time was up and we looked down we could not see the airfield.

We called Upper Heyford on our R.T. and informed them we were having difficulty identifying their lights amongst all the others. They answered our call saying they could see our navigation lights quite clearly because the aircraft was over the field.

It was a mystery to us because we could not see the lights at all and fuel was getting very low.

Suddenly the Bomb Aimer said he could see them underneath us, and on looking down my eyes focused on a drem system which was very dim compared with the others. I immediately made the landing with a very relieved crew after six and a half hours flying.

At the end of an Operational Training Course it was the practice to select a couple of crews and send them on an actual operation over one of the occupied countries, normally France, to drop leaflets on a specific area, notifying the people of some important event which the Germans had not broadcast. It was called 'Nickelling'.

Our crew was detailed for one of these operations to Alencon in Northern France. The leaflets dropped gave information on important American Air Force raids against the oil wells at Ploesti in Rumania where heavy damage was done; the document also included photographs, taken from the air as the aircraft went in at low level and showed a lot of fires and smoke.

We were somewhat surprised to go on the operation because we thought our first trip would be with a front line Squadron, and there were some dry mouths as we prepared for take off and we suddenly realised 'this is it'.

Our course was south from Bruntingthorpe to a point on the south coast before crossing to France.

As we flew south over England my thoughts were on our experience, here I was twenty years of age, Captain and Pilot of a Wellington Bomber flying a crew on an operation on which we had no idea what to expect from the enemy defences, or how to deal with them.

I was asking myself such questions as 'How do I judge the distance from an anti aircraft shell burst' or will the gunners pick up a fighter attack before he starts firing at us.

When we were over the Channel and looked towards France I saw spasmodic shell bursts and the odd searchlight as it probed the sky.

I was expecting a fighter attack anytime and told the gunners to keep searching below ; that is where most attacks came from.

The French blackout wasn't very good and the odd light was flashed at us, some of them with the 'V' in Morse and we realised they still thought themselves as allies.

The Bomb Aimer dropped the leaflets out of a chute north of Alencon to allow for wind direction and speed ; after which we turned for home.

As soon as I had turned the aircraft the Rear Gunner shouted "fighter" startling all of us and I expected tracer bullets to hit the aircraft. However nothing happened and evidently he had seen the lights of an aerodrome come into view as I completed the turn, and mistaken them for a fighter.

The rest of the trip was uneventful and we arrived back at base four and a half hours after take off. The rest of the crews asked questions about our first operation which made us feel like veterans.

L'Amérique en Guerre

LE 11 AOUT 1943   No. 62

SICILE : La libération totale de l'ile approche

VOIR PAGE 2

RUSSIE : L'Armée Rouge reprend Orel et Bielgorod

VOIR PAGE 2

ALLEMAGNE : Goebbels dit aux Berlinois " Partez ! "

VOIR PAGE 2

PACIFIQUE : Les Japonais sont chassés de Munda

VOIR PAGE 4

Cent soixante-dix-sept Liberators ont attaqué les installations pétrolières de Ploesti en Roumanie le 1er août. Préparé par le général américain L. H. Brereton, Commandant de la 9ème Force de l'U.S.A.A.F., le raid a été couronné de succès. Il s'agissait d'atteindre en plein ce centre d'où l'Allemagne tire presque le tiers de ses produits pétrolifères. Les dégâts causés ont été considérables. Ci-dessous, un bombardier lourd, se dessinant sur la fumée noire du pétrole en flammes, survole de très bas les raffineries de Ploesti.

Ploesti en flammes

Copy of leaflets dropped by our crew over France on operation from OTU.

Chapter 5

No. 1661 Conversion Unit, Winthorpe, Newark

At the end of August 1943 the crew was posted to No. 1661 Conversion Unit at Winthorpe, Newark to fly Lancasters.

The Mid Upper Gunner, Jock Jameson, from Aberdeen had joined us at O.T.U., and Johnny Harris, Flight Engineer from Biggleswade, Beds. came to us at Winthorpe which made up the crew to seven, the compliment of a Lancaster.

My screen pilot was F/O Dorehill a Rhodesian who had flown on a low level attack to Augsburg with 44 Rhodesian Squadron earlier in the War, it was led by W/C Nettleton who was decorated with the Victoria Cross.

There is a sequel to F/O Dorehill being my 'Screen' at Winthorpe.

Thirty years after, one of my nephews who is now a Captain with British Airways was a First Officer on Tridents and we were both attending the wedding of another nephew.

He had brought his log book with him and as we compared the contents of his book with mine, he noticed the name Dorehill and said they had a Captain on British Airways who was due to retire in a few weeks.

I asked him if he knew Dorehill's Christian name, and he said "Pat" the same Christian name as the Officer I knew. My nephew said he would be flying with Captain Dorehill within the next few days and would ask him about his Wartime service.

The next time I saw my nephew he said it was the same Dorehill who remembered our flights together, quite a coincidence.

Before flying the Lancaster for the first time I did three hours flying on Manchesters which was the prototype of the Lancasters ; but as it could not maintain height on one engine, was taken off operations. I believe many of them were lost because of this weakness.

The Lancaster was a beautiful aircraft to fly ; definitely a pilot's aeroplane ; it handled very lightly, could reach heights of 22,000 (feet) fully loaded and could even maintain height on two engines.

It had no vices, except for a slight swing to port on take off, and was nearly impossible to stall. If you put her in a stall position with nose up, the air speed would just about disappear before the nose gently dropped, not a vicious wing drop like the Oxford.

Now that we had a full crew a lot of night exercises were flown at Conversion Unit using 'G' a Navigational Aid, and also fighter affiliation with Spitfires during daylight.

Because the Lancaster was so light on the controls it was possible to turn inside a fighter during a corkscrew, which was Bomber Command's main evasive action against German night fighters.

The last night exercise of the Conversion Course was one of six hours and covered a number of towns, it also included a dummy mining run over Cardigan Bay but this was abandoned after three Lancasters crashed into the Welsh mountains on consecutive nights as they descended to fly over the bay.

Chapter 6

No. 106 Squadron No. 5 Group Bomber Command

At the beginning of October 1943 we were ready to join an Operational Squadron and were posted to No. 106 Squadron 5 Group stationed at Syerston between Newark and Nottingham.

We were placed in 'B' Flight which flew twelve aircraft the same as 'A' Flight.

The Squadron originally operated against enemy shipping but its main task in 1943 was the bombing of Germany ; however there was always a Naval Liaison Officer attached to it.

"Our first two weeks were taken up with cross countries, practice bombing and 'circuits and bumps'."

"One night we were despatched with another crew to Bottesford to do circuits and bumps; we were the only two aircraft on the circuit so everything went smoothly, as one aircraft took off the other would be on the downwind leg".

However after one landing, I was taxiing round for the next take off but could not see the lights of the other aircraft, which should have been on a downwind leg.

I soon found out what had happened as we proceeded round the perimeter track ; I saw the tail light of the other Lancaster in front of me and knew it was stood.

I stopped the aircraft and waited, but the other one didn't move forward. After a short time one of my crew left the aircraft and went forward to see what had happened.

When he returned he said that a N.A.A.F.I. wagon had stopped on the perimeter track to supply the night duty ground crew, and the other pilot of the Lancaster had not seen it, because it did not have any lights and he continued taxiing. The van had become fast under the Lancaster's belly and of course it could not move ; this left the pilot mystified why his aircraft wasn't moving.

Evidently when the ladies in the van, who were serving food to the ground crew, saw the huge machine bearing down on their little van, they fled.

Who could blame them.

Operation-Leipzig 20th October 1943

(I received my commission 2 hours before taking off on this operation)

On October 20th 1943 the crew were put on the Squadron Battle Order for our first trip - target Leipzig - and what a trip it turned out to be.

We took off in Lancaster D V 297 and climbed to 20,000 ft.

We had no trouble on the first part of the trip but the weather over Germany was appalling, with cumulus clouds reaching over 20,000 ft, and we were frequently flying in and out of the tops in icing conditions.

COMBAT REPORT

1. On the night of October 20/21 Lancaster 'O' of 106 Squadron detailed to attack LEIPZIG sighted a twin engined unidentified aircraft when over D.R. position 52° 05N. 12° 35E.

2. The Lancaster at the time (2053 hours) was at 20,000 feet flying on a course of 161° N at an I.A.S. of 155 m.p.h. The first indication was 'Monica' pips being recorded, and shortly afterwards the Mid Upper Gunner sighted the t/e/a/c on port quarter up at 600 yards. The Lancaster pilot, Pilot Officer Starkey was instructed to dive port and at the same time the Mid Upper Gunner opened fire with a long burst. At this stage the Rear Gunner also sighted the e/a but before he could bring his guns to bear it disappeared into the clouds on the starboard quarter up.

3. No unusual phenomenon was noticed, and owing to 9 tenths cloud at 19,000 feet, the question of searchlights did not arise, although visibility above clouds was good.

4. Approximately 300 rounds were expended by the M/U Gunner without stoppages and no return fire was experienced from the e/a.

5. No damage is claimed to the e/a which carried no lights and approached from the light part of the sky.
   R/G 1431392 Sgt. Ellick. 7A.G.S. 29 OTU.
   M/U 1007433 Sgt. Jamieson. 2 A.G.S. 29 OTU.

Flight Lieutenant For S/Ldr. Commanding No. 106 Squadron. R.A.F.

Combat report against a German twin Nightfighter on Leipzig raidOctober 1943

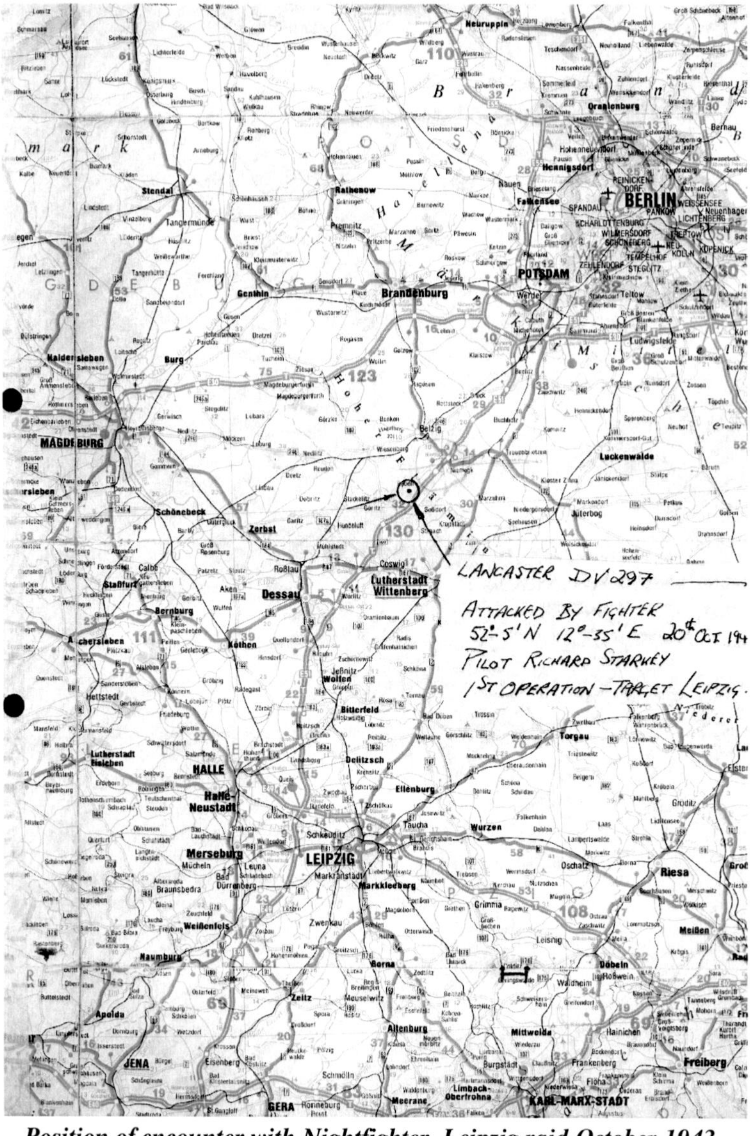
LANCASTER DV297
ATTACKED BY FIGHTER
52°-5'N 12°-35'E 20th OCT 194
PILOT RICHARD STARKEY
1ST OPERATION - TARGET LEIPZIG.
BERLIN
POTSDAM
Brandenburg
MAGDEBURG
Dessau
Lutherstadt Wittenberg
HALLE
LEIPZIG
Torgau
Jüterbog
Luckenwalde

Position of encounter with Nightfighter, Leipzig raid October 1943

About half way to the target the airspeed indicator suddenly dropped off the 'clock', this left us in an awkward situation and I had to fly on

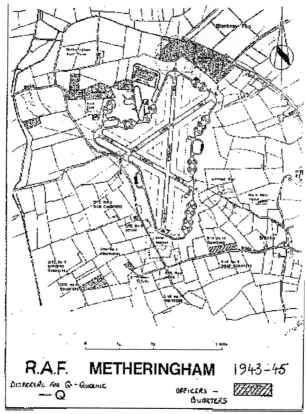

R.A.F. METHERINGHAM 1943-45

DISPERSAL FOR Q - QUEENIE
— Q

OFFICERS —
QUARTERS

Layout plan of Metheringham airfield

other instruments to maintain the aircraft in a normal flying position. It reminded me of the Air Force adage - 'There I was at 20,000 ft with sweet **** on the clock'.

This is where I needed my instrument flying training, because the airspeed indicator was very important during corkscrewing which was our main evasive action against fighters.

At this point of the operation 'Monica' pips (advanced warning of aircraft approaching - either friendly or enemy) were recorded and the Mid Upper Gunner instructed me to dive port. He had sighted a twin-engined aircraft which appeared out of the clouds as we also emerged. He quickly gave the evasion order, then fired a burst at the enemy aircraft before it disappeared into the clouds.

It must have been a shock to the night fighter pilot when tracer bullets flashed past his aircraft, but under the conditions he could not do much about it.

Metheringham airfield looking South

Metheringham airfield looking East, remains of control tower in distance

Remains of control tower Meteringham

Aircrew at an open day at Metheringham Heritage centre

On route the searchlights were ineffective because of cloud thickness and still without the airspeed indicator we bombed on E.T.A. at a large glow on the clouds which we took to be the target.

The return journey was uneventful but the appalling weather conditions did not improve until we descended over the North Sea and air temperature increased ; the airspeed came back on the 'clock' much to my relief.

All aircrew were allowed nine days leave every six weeks. During the six weeks they might fly twelve operations and during the winter of 1943 /44 the bad weather was the main reason for 'stand downs' ; also we did not operate during the 'moon' period which ran from four days before to four days after full moon ; so eight operations was a good average. Several crews took leave during the moon period, leaving a few crews to operate, if required, on specific targets, probably in Unoccupied Countries.

On 11th November 1943 106 Squadron moved to Metheringham in East Lincolnshire, about fifteen miles south east of Lincoln. At that time a few stations in 5 Group were situated around Newark and Nottingham and it was decided to move Squadrons east near the East Coast and The Wash.

Metheringham formed a base with Woodhall Spa (No. 617 Squadron) and Coningsby (No. 619 and one other Squadron).

The Squadron arrived at Metheringham just as the 'Berlin Season' was about to start and over the next four months several crews would be lost.

However small things occurred which go beyond belief and I will describe such a situation at Metheringham. Although the Flying Personnel and Ground Crew from 106 at Syerston were transferred to Metheringham, the Administrative Staff including the Station Commander, a Group Captain, came from Bottesford.

In the Officers' Mess Squadrons' aircrew outnumbered the Administrative Staff and as both parties had used different methods for settling mess bills at their previous stations, a meeting was held to decide by majority which method to adopt.

Naturally as there were more aircrew, our method of paying for drinks as they were ordered was adopted against the Administrative Staffs' practice of putting everything on a Mess bill and settling at the end of the month.

This would have meant relatives of missing aircrew settling their bills.

The only reason I am writing this is because the Station Commander said afterwards he would hold both Flight Commanders responsible if the practice didn't work. A childish thing to say when the aircrew by majority preferred the system and had seen it operate satisfactorily. What an attitude on a front line Bomber Station.

As it was the Station Commander was never enthusiastic about the Squadron and vetoed any immediate recommendations for decorations to aircrew.

Conditions at Metheringham were far different to Syerston, which was a peace time station with permanent buildings and fixtures, whereas Metheringham was a War Time Aerodrome with many Nissen huts, situated on the edge of the Fens and in November could be foggy and cold.

There were six Officers to one Nissan hut on the Officer Aircrew site ; the other occupants were two other pilots from my flight, a Bomb Aimer and Navigator from the same crew, and an Administrative Officer from Station Headquarters.

I remember on nights when we were stood down the five aircrew occupants would sit round a stove and discuss their reaction if shot down by a fighter. Although all of us had seen many bombers meeting that fate we could only surmise the conditions in the aircraft as they dived helplessly out of control to the ground.

The Bomb Aimer said that as he was more or less lying on the escape hatch in the nose of the aircraft he would abandon it without difficulty, he hoped, when the pilot gave the order.

The three pilots more or less accepted what would be their fate because of extreme odds against their survival, having to try and control the aircraft whilst the crew bailed out. The Navigator just hoped he could get to an escape hatch.

This then was the topic of conversation on those nights in the middle of the Battle of Berlin when the odds were very much against survival.

The Bomb Aimer and Navigator would later be shot down and I and my crew would also be lost on a later raid.

If the Squadron wasn't operating various exercises were flown during the day including navigating and blind bombing by H²s which were fitted to all aircraft between January and March 1944. Blind bombing targets from 10,000ft were made on various cities in England with the Navigator and Wireless Operator working together on H²s and instructing the Bomb Aimer when to operate the camera on a ' bomb run'. The photographs indicated successful attacks on the majority of runs.

On some days I would take the opportunity to 'beat up' my home town of Barnsley and the Lancaster became a familiar sight as I flew low level, about 300ft above the ground making a pass over my home where there would be many tablecloths waving in the vicinity.

On one occasion, 9th February 1944, I did a low level across the town passing over the Town Hall at about 200ft. As I flew over I noticed quite a crowd in front of the building and my Rear Gunner confirmed this as we left the town behind. Later that night I telephoned home and my Dad asked me if it was my aircraft that had flown low over the Town Hall. I said yes and asked him why there was a crowd. He said the King and Queen had been visiting and had just come out of the Town Hall as the Lancaster passed over ; everyone thought it was a salute to Their Majesties.

In those days there was no publicity if they were to make a visit to a locality.

My crew made friends with some of the Land Army girls who lived in a Hostel in the village of Martin on the outskirts of the airfield.

Our first meeting with them was on the first Sunday after we moved to Metheringham. The Squadron was not operating that night and the weather was typical November Fen weather, foggy and drizzly.

We were not aware there was a Land Army Hostel nearby and rang Telephone Enquiries to ask if there was one in the district. We were told it was right next to the Telephone Kiosk we were using and gave us the number.

We rang them and from that moment our social life, when we were not operating, was taken care of, with some of the nicest girls (several from Yorkshire) I had met. There could be no serious relationships because of our work, crews were regularly going missing and a lot of them had boyfriends in the Services.

I shall always remember the dances in the Village Hall at Timberlands, a nearby village, on Saturday nights, when we could make it.

The Station Dance Band would play, and before walking to the dance from Martin we would meet in the local pub in the village and have a few drinks in the 'Nook'. These girls were very kind and if their work started at around the same time as we landed from a raid some of them would be waiting near the dispersal over the boundary to see if we had returned safely, and when I came on leave there was always something to bring with me, i.e. eggs.

In June 1997 I returned to Timberlands and met Mr. & Mrs. P.Mason, who were teenagers at that time.

The Village Hall is still the same, and they told me some of the girls had met and married local boys and were living in the area.

My Flight Commander on 106 completed two tours early in 1944 and was waiting to be posted, when one day he sent for me and said " you think you can fly these Lancasters, well I'm going to show you how one should be flown, so let us go out to your aircraft". I said I would get the crew together but was told not to bother there would just be the two of us flying it.

When we arrived at dispersal and entered the aircraft he sat in the pilot's seat and I stood by his side to do the Flight Engineers duties.

After taxiing to the end of the runway he looked at his watch and opened the throttles, the aircraft quickly picked up speed and he was soon airborne, immediately starting a climbing turn which brought him to the down wind leg at 500ft where he levelled out.

As the runway disappeared under the wing he turned and dived to port ; since taking off he had lifted the flaps only when required but not fully because he was soon ready to lower them again ; he had raised the wheels during the climbing turn and put them down again just before he dived towards the runway. He lowered the rest of the flaps on the short run in and touched down 45 seconds after becoming airborne, it was some flying with marvellous control.

As we taxied off the runway he told me to change seats and do exactly as he did in the same time - if I could.

Our crew had completed around eighteen operations at the time and I was a competent pilot of a Lancaster, especially our own, which we were flying. I knew I could do a 'split harse' circuit but wasn't sure I could beat his time ; the result of my endeavour was a 60 seconds circuit, with which I was satisfied, but he said laughingly "I would never be as good as him".

However I could then side slip a Lancaster to lose height and this helped my time.

This Flight Commander when the Squadron operated from Syerston, where there was a valley at the end of one runway through which the River Trent ran, took off on that runway with a full load of bombs and petrol, but lost an engine just after take off and disappeared into the valley at the end of the runway whilst trying to maintain height. I am told that everyone watching expected one big explosion as he hit the valley floor, but the aircraft came into view, staggering to climb to sufficient height, to complete a circuit and landing.

He struggled to maintain height on the down wind leg and managed to turn on the approach to land with the bombs, (he never had sufficient height to jettison). The landing was made successfully on what was a great feat of flying.

During February we had a Squadron photograph taken in front of a Lancaster one afternoon, after which our crew was to carry out an H^2s exercise taking photographs of Peterborough Railway Station, lasting two hours.

I knew there was not enough time to complete the exercise before dark if the Squadron photo session was a long one. It turned out that we were left insufficient time to complete our flying exercise in daylight and advised our new Flight Commander from Training Command of the situation.

He ordered me to take off and do the exercise, this was typical of Training Command attitude, especially someone who had just been transferred to a Squadron, there was no flexibility.

Another crew captained by an Australian were detailed to do an H^2s exercise, similar to ours, over Derby, but we agreed to report 10/10ths cloud over the cities and return immediately.

We arrived over Peterborough with clear skies but would have had no chance to complete twelve photo runs before dark. The light wasn't

38

very good but I decided to do some low flying as there was little chance of being identified.

The Bomb Aimer and Navigator took up positions in the nose of the aircraft to enjoy the ride and we were soon down to 50ft over the flat countryside when I noticed a railway bridge in front of us with a policeman riding a bicycle across it. We roared over him and when we had passed the Rear Gunner, who could not see the bridge until we passed it, said a policeman was picking himself up from his bicycle which had fallen over. It was a case of letting off steam, first of all for the Flight Commander's attitude and secondly we operated over Germany at 20-25,000ft and any opportunity to get away with a bit of low flying, we took it.

Incidentally many years after the War I learned that the Australian Pilot was killed in a car accident in New South Wales where he was Head of the Horseracing Board in that State.

Another practice which was popular with the crew was air to sea firing off Skegness, when a lead marker was dropped in the sea and all gun turrets were used to fire at it. I do not know if it benefited the gunners but it gave us all a lot of fun because I flew the aircraft just above the waves which left four lanes of disrupted water as the propellers spun just above the tops.

We finished the exercise by continuing low level towards the Clock Tower on the sea front, climbing quickly about 400yds from the shore.

On one occasion when we did the exercise I chose an area of the sea two miles North of Skegness and when the manoeuvre ended turned the aircraft toward land at wave top height. As we quickly approached the shore I realised we were heading straight for Butlins Holiday Camp which was taken over for training by the Royal Navy for the duration of the War.

I could see the sailors queuing for dinner and decided to give them an 'appetiser' so flew the Lancaster at around 100ft over their heads. Unfortunately a high ranking Naval Officer was visiting the establishment and took a dim view ; someone identified the aircraft letters and next day I was on the carpet before the Squadron Commander, for dangerous flying.

When I told him we were air to sea firing at low level and came towards land, I started my climb just off shore but was still at a low altitude when I passed over the Camp. I remember he smiled and ordered me not to repeat the practice again, but as I was already climbing over the Camp would take no further action.

Frankfurt - 20th December 1943

Our third operation was to Frankfurt on the 20th December 1943, the second had been to Berlin at the commencement of the Battle of Berlin, which opened in November.

We took off for Frankfurt in aircraft JB 534. My Mid-Upper Gunner had been granted compassionate leave, and his replacement was a Sergeant, whose crew had already completed their first tour and he had to complete his last trip by flying with other crews.

We had no trouble on the outward journey and flew at 21,000ft. The target was covered by a lot of cloud so the ground markers were hidden and I also remember that the Germans had lit a decoy fire south of the City.

About ten miles north of the Target on our return journey, we were fired upon by cannons and machine gun fire from what we presumed was a night fighter, the Rear Gunner immediately instructed me to corkscrew as enemy tracer came from the port quarter. I did so and after one complete corkscrew resumed normal course.

I could tell we had been hit around the port main plane and prayed we would not catch fire. However after breaking off the first attack the Fighter attacked again almost immediately and the aircraft was hit again. I corkscrewed but no Fighter was sighted by either Gunner so we resumed course. The Fighter was never seen and although the Rear Gunner attempted to open fire on three occasions, his guns failed to function.

When we resumed course it was evident that the aircraft had been severely damaged because it started to shudder violently and I had great difficulty controlling it. The vibration transferred to my body as I fought to maintain control.

The Rear Gunner reported that the port fin and tailplane rudder was extensively damaged and a large part had disappeared. As for the main plane we could not see any damage but knew there was some.

Soon after the attack the Navigator instructed me to change course, but on applying rudder and aileron the aircraft began to bank steeply and I had to put her back on an even keel by using automatic pilot - manual controls were ineffective. The shuddering continued over the North Sea and I gave instructions to prepare for any eventuality.

However we managed to remain airborne and after approximately two and three quarter hours we approached Base.

The Wireless Operator informed the Control Tower of the condition of the aircraft and that it was essential to make a right hand circuit, and also that we must land immediately.

Permission was given to circuit at a height of 800ft and other aircraft were ordered to maintain their height until we landed.

On our approach down the funnel of the drem system we began to drift to starboard and I dare not counteract this because to make a turning to port would have been a disaster. After an anxious couple of minutes we touched down on the grass in darkness fifty yards to the right of the flare path, and as the Mid Upper Gunner left the aircraft he knelt down and kissed the ground, having completed a memorable 30th operation.

COMBAT REPORT

1. On the night of 20th-21st December 1943, Lancaster 'O' of 106 Squadron was fired upon by what was presumed to be cannons and machine gun from a fighter.

2. The Rear Gunner, who was at the time searching to starboard quarter, immediately instructed his Captain, Pilot Officer Starkey, to corkscrew port, as enemy tracer appeared to come mostly from the port quarter. No enemy fighter was again observed, and after one complete corkscrew manoeuvre, the Lancaster resumed normal course. Almost immediately a second burst was experienced and hits were registered on the Lancaster's port fin and rudder and also on port main plane.

3. Once again the Lancaster corkscrewed port but no fighter was sighted by either gunner. The Lancaster once more resumed original course after one complete manoeuvre of the corkscrew and no further trouble was experienced. The Lancaster at the time, 2009 hours, was flying at 23,000 feet on a course of 285° N. at an I.A.S. of 135 m.p.h. The position was 50° 30N., 06° 50E on the homeward journey from Frankfurt.

4. The Rear Gunner reports that although he attempted to open fire on at least three occasions, his guns failed to function. The guns were inspected the following morning and were found to be serviceable, and it is assumed that the oil in the palmer firing mechanism had become frozen.

5. 'Monica' was unserviceable and had been so throughout the flight.

6. Visibility was good, seven tenths cloud at 10,000 feet.

7. No searchlight activity was noticed but a number of fighter flares were visible to starboard at same level as Lancaster.

R/Gunner 1431392   Sgt.Ellick.M
                      (No. 7 A.G.S. and No. 29 O.T.U.)

M/Gunner 1398602   Sgt. Johnson N.H.
                      (No. 4 A.G.S. and No. 14 O.T.U.)

Flight Lieutenant
for Wing Commander Commanding
No. 106 Squadron. R.A.F.

Squadron Commander's Remarks
No Comment

Station Commander's Remarks
No claim is made.

(signed) W.N. McKechnie.
Group Captain Commanding
R.A.F. Station, Metheringham.

Combat report with Nightfighter on the Frankfurt raid December 1943

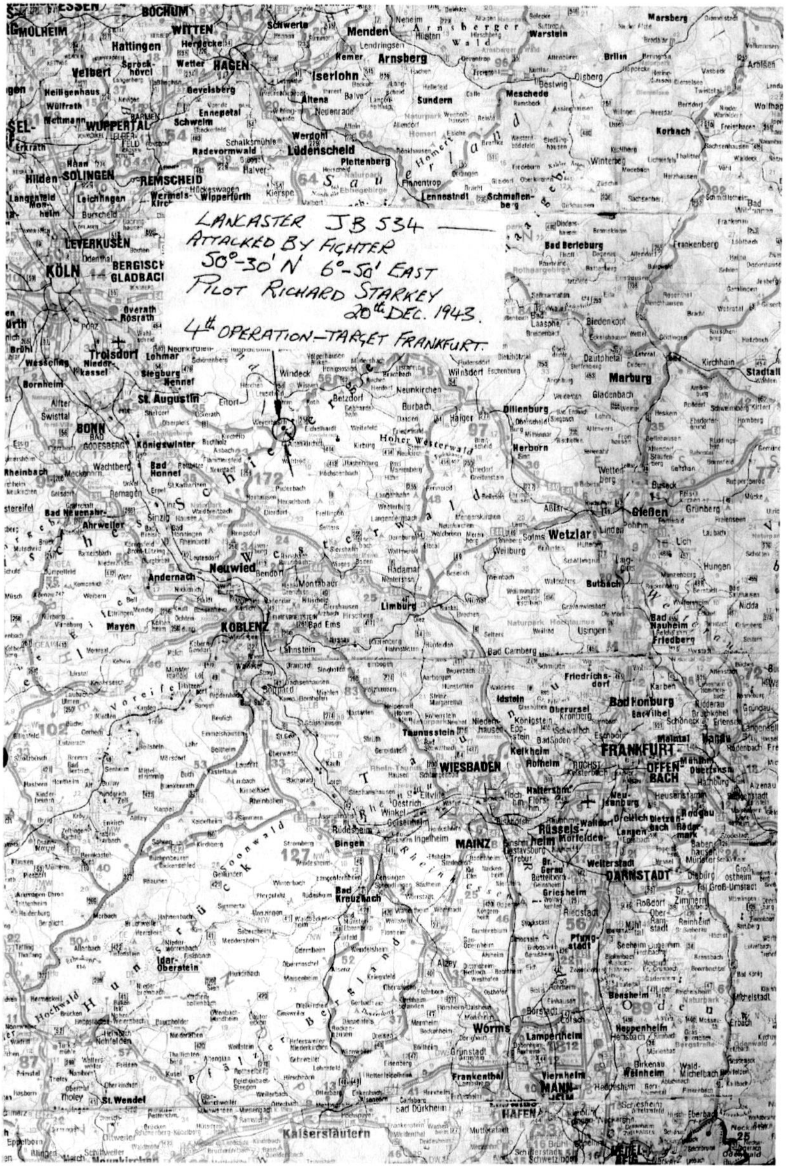
LANCASTER JB 534 —
ATTACKED BY FIGHTER
50°-30' N 6°-50' EAST
PILOT RICHARD STARKEY
20th DEC. 1943.
4th OPERATION—TARGET FRANKFURT.
KÖLN
BONN
KOBLENZ
WIESBADEN
MAINZ
FRANKFURT
DARMSTADT
Marburg
Gießen
Wetzlar
Limburg
Neuwied
Worms
Kaiserslautern

Position of Nightfighter attack North of Frankfurt

When the aircraft was examined next morning, the full extent of the damage was revealed. There was severe damage to the port fin and rudder, more than fifty percent was missing, the port side of the fuselage had been riddled with bullets which stopped just before the Wireless Operator's position but had gone through the Mid Upper Gunner's legs.

Material covering the port aileron had been ripped off and most frightening of all a cannon shell had exploded on the underside of the port mainplane creating a jagged hole approximately one foot in diameter. If the shell had exploded further forward it would have hit the fuel tanks and the aircraft would have 'gone up'.

Repairs had to be carried out on the airfield by workmen from Avros, and took approximately six weeks to complete. Three months ago I contacted Mr.H.Homes who keeps records of every Lancaster manufactured by Avros.

Unfortunately he was not able to enlighten me as to which parts had been replaced because records were no longer available. However he did tell me that 1,171 man hours were employed on the aircraft in order to bring it back to operational standard.

Aircraft JB 534 was transferred to 'A' flight after the repairs were completed, only to crash on Timberlands Fell near the airfield when returning from its first operation after repairs, killing all the crew except one.

Our Squadron was a Path Finder support Squadron which meant on certain raids a couple of crews were selected to take off before the rest of the Squadron and fly ahead of the Path Finders dropping 'window' (small strips of material) from the aircraft to fuzz the enemies radar, where following aircraft could fly.

One other crew besides ours was detailed for a supporting role on another raid to Frankfurt.

We took off in broad daylight ; darkness was due to fall about the time we were due over the South Coast, (we were taking a Southerly route) on the way to France before altering course for Frankfurt ; but when we approached our point of departure from England although the light was fading it was still too bright for our operation.

However daylight soon faded as we crossed the Channel and as we arrived over the French Coast darkness had fallen. We had no window protection because the two of us were ahead of the Path Finders and had to be very alert for Fighters, anti aircraft fire and searchlights.

Our trip went smoothly but it was strange to be the first aircraft over a city before a raid. After flying through heavy flak we dropped the bombs by H^2s, took photographs and returned to Base thankful we had not suffered any damage.

The other crew had more excitement because after they dropped their bombs there was a massive explosion on the ground, they said they had never seen anything like it.

When their photographs were developed back at Base, these were done on an overlapping basis, whatever they had hit showed as a white flash about 3" square and Intelligence thought they may have scored a direct hit on an ammunition factory situated on an island in the river.

I flew to Frankfurt in 1998 and as we approached the airport saw an island in the River Main which had a chemical installation. This island was the one my colleague hit.

One of our pilots, an Australian, returned from an operation one night saying his Lancaster had been turned over by a near miss from an anti aircraft shell. He was over Holland on the way to the target with his bomb load when the incident happened.

None of the other pilots in the Flight had been affected by such an incident and we asked him how he got out of it. He evidently pulled the control column back, this was because it reversed its' role as the aircraft was upside down, and it dropped nose heavy like a stone ; the pressure on the aircraft must have been terrific and it took him and the Flight Engineer all their strength to pull it out of the dive.

It certainly proved the Lancaster was a great aircraft because no structural damage occurred.

Most Wartime Bomber airfields had three runways ; two of 2,000yds in length and one of 1600yds, the latter was only used when the wind was in line with it. One of the 2,000 yard runways at Metheringham was generally used because of the prevailing wind.

For dark take offs at night a line of lights, like cats eyes, had been installed across the runway 800yds from the end to give pilots a guide to the distance remaining for take off ; these were very important because getting a Lancaster off the ground, fully loaded with bombs and petrol was a mouth drying experience as the end of the runway rushed toward you, the last thing you would want or remember was an engine failure. The take off after straightening the Lancaster on the runway was started by holding the aircraft tightly on the brakes and pushing all four throttles fully open. The aircraft would start moving forward, and you gradually released the brakes, at the same time pushing the control column fully forward in order to get the tail up as quickly as possible and build up speed.

At that point the Flight Engineer would operate the throttles by pushing them through 'the gate' to get extra boost, this could only be maintained for two minutes before he brought them back to normal maximum revs.

The two minutes would give us time to get into the air as I concentrated on lifting her off the ground, meanwhile the Engineer would call the speed out as it slowly built up - 90... 100... 110 mph, at which point I started easing it off the ground, which sometimes it was reluctant to leave and by that time we had left the 800yds marker well behind and were thundering towards the end of the flarepath. You were then fully

44

Lancaster "Q" Queenie in Dispersal with crew

Mid Upper Gunner	Jock	
Rear Gunner	Joe	George
Wireless Operator		Wally
Bomb Aimer		Colin
Navigator		
Pilot	Self	
Flight Engineer	Johnny	

committed and had no chance if you had to cancel take off, it would be the aircraft and the crew.

I remember waiting to take off one night when two bright flashes lit up the sky as two Lancasters exploded at nearby airfields - no doubt crashing due to engine failure.

At 120 mph the wheels came off the ground and as the speed built up I would start a flatish climbing turn out of the drem system with the inner wing barely 50ft off the ground. Sometimes I left our drem system with insufficient speed to turn and would approach another airfields' system nearby who were also dispatching aircraft, so we had to be very alert and keep clear of their aircraft.

As the altitude increased very slowly I brought the aircraft round to fly over the Airfield and set course given to me by the Navigator. We would leave the Coast at Skegness, if we were flying straight to Berlin, and then the Bomb Aimer would fuse the bombs and I would turn off the navigation lights.

The first part of the flight was over the North Sea and, apart from flashes on the water as some crews jettisoned their bombs, it was hard to believe there were 800 Bombers all closely flying in a stream approximately ten miles long and five miles wide.

'Monica' was continually picking up approaching aircraft which alerted the crew to locate them visually, and it was usually another Lancaster which would slide across the sky above us, probably 50ft higher, silhouetted against the stars with exhaust emitting blue flame from under the cowlings.

When the Bomber stream approached Texel Island the Germans put up their usual flak barrage with some success.

No Bomber Command story would be complete without a reference to Texal Island near the German Coast in the North Sea.

In the winter of 1943/44 the route to Berlin and other cities sometimes took us near the Island, with its many anti aircraft gun emplacements firing heavily at the Bomber stream.

As we neared the Island, crews knew a few would not survive the onslaught and waited for the inevitable ; this happened when four or five aircraft exploded as they were hit with full bomb loads and flaming parts of aircraft spun down to hit the ground and spread a trail of fire.

Any ex Bomber Command aircrew operating at that time would agree that a special raid ought to have been made on the Island to take out as many guns as possible.

Oboe

During the raids on the Ruhr 'OBOE' (carried by mosquito Path Finder aircraft) was a radio bombing instrument using pulses to determine distances from two ground stations, and was very accurate.

The aircraft flew at a constant range from one ground station and when at the correct range from another ground station, the latter station sent the order for the aircraft to drop its markers or bombs.

Other Path Finder aircraft dropped their markers on the first ones and the Main Force then came in to bomb.

Berlin 24th March 1944

Bomber Command suffered its heaviest losses during the Battle of Berlin on the night of 24th March 1944 when seventy four aircraft were lost.

Our crew operated that night and the following is my description of the raid.

The outward route was over the North Sea to Denmark then south-east over the Baltic Sea crossing the German Coast and continuing south-east before turning south through the Target.

The trip was to be one of the worst we encountered because of the strong winds. On the way out over the North Sea the Navigator was finding winds with speeds far in excess of those in his Flight Plan and coming from a more northerly direction than predicted at Briefing.

We were 'wind finders' that night and I remember the Navigator advising me that the wind speed was unbelievable - approaching 100mph and should he broadcast his findings back to Bomber Command. I said if he was satisfied with his calculations he must transmit them back to England.

A number of aircraft were detailed as windfinders on every raid, and when the Navigators had calculated the actual wind speed and velocity they were transmitted back where an average wind speed was calculated from those sent back by aircraft and then relayed to the Bomber Force to use on their journey.

I ordered my Navigator to work from his own calculations and ignore the wind speeds being sent back to us because they were far too low.

By the time the Danish Coast was crossed we were many miles south of track as a result of the high wind speed from the north. At that time nobody had heard of the Jet Stream, but many years after the raid and on reflection, Bomber Command met this phenomenon on that night.

The Force was scattered over a very wide front as we approached Berlin well before zero hour.

Some Captains ordered their Navigators to work to the winds broadcast from England, and found themselves hopelessly off track ; others navigated on their own findings and were reaching points well in advance of E.T.A. but they were not as far off course as the others.

We arrived over the Target early and I decided to risk going round the City on the eastern side, by which time the P.F.F. markers would be going down and we could start our bombing run.

The activity in the sky over the City was awesome and frightening, as were all raids on Berlin.

The sky was full of sparkling flashes as anti-aircraft shells from twelve hundred guns burst in a box barrage which was sent up every two minutes, containing the equivalent of an ammunition dump.

I estimated that anyone getting through that would be very lucky indeed especially as the aircraft had to be flown straight and level with bomb doors open during the bombing run and take photographs after dropping the bombs. There were also hundreds of searchlights, making two cones over the City which the bombers had to try and evade.

The Fighters no longer waited outside the perimeter of the Target where they were in little danger from their own flak, because we were now severely damaging their Cities. They flew amongst us in this area of death ignoring their own safety, meeting the anti-aircraft fire in order to get amongst us, and many a bomber was shot down when most vulnerable with bomb doors open.

When we were on our bombing run with two other Lancasters, whose Bomb Aimers had chosen the same markers as my Bomb Aimer, a twin engined Fighter flew past our nose with cannon and machine guns firing at one of the Lancasters ; there were tracers flying all over the sky as my Gunners and the others in the third aircraft joined the targeted Lancaster to return the fire.

However we lost another aircraft that night as the stricken Lancaster turned over on its back and went down in flames ; we did not see anyone escaping because we were concentrating on the bombing run.

The Luftwaffe were now using single-engined Fighters in the battle, generally over the target and as I took a quick glance down at the fires I saw twelve of them circling up line astern towards the Bombers whose bellies were red from the reflection of the flames below.

The searchlight cones held two Bombers like moths round a candle ; the pilots were tossing their aircraft all over the sky but they were held like stage artists in a spot light. The next move was from the Fighters who came in and inflicted the coup de grace, the Bombers plunging down in flames before exploding and cascading in balls of fire to splash among the inferno below.

A pilot had to take whatever action he could to get across the Target Area, and one practice was to fly near a coned aircraft and hope the action against it would help him get across. This wasn't always possible because although the brightness was less intense they could be seen.

When a raid was at its peak with eight hundred aircraft bombing in a twenty minute period, the illuminations had to be seen to be believed. The Target indicators red and green chandeliers two hundred feet in length cascaded down with a shimmering brightness, flak was bursting, filling every part of the sky with twinkling bursts, and as you flew towards them there was no escape ; you thought you would never get through it.

Many years afterwards I read in a book that a Bomb Aimer who flew on the raid was so awed by the experience, he just repeated :-

"Jesus Skipper - look at that flak- just look at it
We'll never get through it - just look at it".

That summed it up perfectly.

After bombing the target I gained height to 25,000ft and with relief at surviving the anti aircraft, searchlights and night fighter defences, but we had another fight on our hands before we reached England. The strong head winds and night fighters who had not finished with us.

It soon became apparent that our ground speed was very slow and we did not appear to be making much progress. As we crawled our way west to the next change of course which was to take us north-west between Hanover and Osnabruck, the Navigator was continuously amending his air plot to try and keep us on course, but we were being blown south of our intended track.

It soon became apparent that the conditions were getting worse and because of the effect of the wind on navigation found ourselves further west than the point where we should have turned north-west to fly between Hanover and Osnabruck. Instead we amended our course to fly between Osnabruck and the Ruhr making sure we kept well clear of the latter area.

We had seen many aircraft shot down since we left Berlin, proof that the force was well scattered and aircraft were being picked off.

As we looked over towards the Ruhr we saw many more, who had wandered over that area, shot down, so they had flown into the two heaviest defended Areas in Germany, Berlin and Ruhr in one night.

I was concentrating our efforts to get to the coast without further trouble when a radar controlled searchlight was suddenly switched on just below the aircraft ; these searchlights had a blue-white beam and more often than not hit the aircraft at the first attempt.

The searchlight crew knew they were near us because the beam started creeping up in front of the aircraft. I put more power on and raised the nose to maintain our position above the beam, but it still continued creeping towards us. I was just on the point of putting the nose down and diving through it when it was switched off - talk about a dry mouth. If the searchlight had found us it would have been joined by others and as was the customary practice a night fighter in the vicinity would have attacked us as we were caught in the beam.

Our last turning point was near the Dutch Border and although our ground speed was very slow the intensity of the defences had slackened off, and for the first time in the raid, fighter activity had ceased. Maybe they had landed to refuel because we were approaching their airfields in Holland.

We did not have any further trouble and eventually reached the North Sea Coast where I pushed down the nose of the aircraft and did a very fast descent to 2,000ft, to the relief of the crew who were thankful to have the raid almost behind us.

As we flew towards the English Coast, the Wireless Operator received a signal ordering us to divert to Wing, an O.T.U. near Luton.

It was a dark night and normally as you approached the coast you saw the odd searchlight but we did not see one light and I was surprised when the Navigator told me, that according to his calculations, we had already crossed the coast ; and gave me a course to Wing. We were by then well inland with navigation lights on flying at 2,000ft but could not see a thing. Suddenly a searchlight switched on to us followed by two more ; they could not have been practising because they could see the lights of our aircraft.

I cursed as they held us, thinking back to the hundreds we had evaded over Germany only to be caught in the beams of a searchlight battery in England.

I was told afterwards that the lights were operated by a crew of A.T.S. girls.

We eventually landed at Wing, after a flight of seven and a half hours on the last big raid to Berlin ; it had been the worst because of the strong winds encountered, which led to the scattering of the Bomber Force assisting enemy night fighters and anti-aircraft batteries to shoot down seventy four Bombers.

Many bombers were diverted to Wing that night, and at breakfast before returning to Metheringham I met the Wing Commander who had given me a Wings Test in Canada. He had been transferred from Training Command and was assembling a crew on Wellingtons at Wing before being converted on to Lancasters. It made me feel quite a veteran with twenty operations completed, and he who had been the Officer in Charge of Training at Swift Current had yet to start.

One little story I can relate occurred during the time of the Battle of Berlin.

When I came home on operational leave I would often visit the local where some of the customers would ask me to take small items back with me to drop on the City. One of these was an ancient pair of pantaloons belonging to a lady named Polly Kirk who was over eighty years of age. She wrote a message on them for 'Adolf' ; I am sure she thought if someone picked them up they would be taken to the Fuhrer ; and as she wrote something less than complimentary she told everyone she had given Hitler a piece of her mind. Anyhow they landed on the 'Big City' so for an old lady the operation was successful.

I have already explained how 'G' worked by sending radio waves out which could be picked up as far as West Belgium to give a reliable ground position. These signals were eagerly awaited on the return journey to show our true position.

50

On this particular night when we came into 'G' range the Navigator took a fix which put us many miles north of track whereas we should have been approaching Northern France. I looked at the heading I was flying on my compass and passed this to the Navigator ; whereupon he said I was flying on a heading 10° more than his plotted one. I asked him to look again and he had mistakenly given me the wrong heading at the last turning point.

I had to make a decision, because I knew we could not reach the right track by turning towards it ; this would mean flying over enemy territory as a solitary aircraft, well out of the Bomber Stream.

We had already left the Main Force some way back ; and on enemy radar our aircraft would be shown as gradually edging towards west north west.

I decided that as we had been lucky not to have been intercepted and as we had only fifty miles to fly to the coast, to continue the heading and hope our luck held.

After crossing the coast and when we were over the North Sea, I instructed the Navigator to give me a course to come in over the East Coast. The effect would be that all Bomber Command, except one aircraft, arriving over the South Coast, and our aircraft would fly in over the East Coast.

We would have to identify ourselves by means of I.F.F. (Identification of Friend or Foe) which had to be used if an aircraft was fifty miles or more off track, so the Wireless Operator switched it on immediately ; also when we were well away from the enemy coast I switched on the navigation lights and hoped we did not meet a 'trigger happy friendly night fighter'.

However we did not see another aircraft and arrived safely at Base.

As Captain I was held responsible for the Navigator's error but under operational pressure these could be made and fortunately we got away with it.

There was also another R.T. system which operated for aircraft who were lost between dusk and dawn. It was called 'Darky' and helped the pilot by giving him his position. He had to call 'Hello Darky' three times and give his identification, only then would the nearest airfield reply to his call ; but if he did not give an identification, no matter how many times he called, he would not receive a reply.

It was also pointless in calling 'Darky' between dawn and dusk.

There was a case in 1943 of an American pilot who had recently arrived in England and was on a map reading exercise over the country which was different to America where roads ran east and west, and north and south, which was a great help in navigation, and he became hopelessly lost.

Although he was flying during daytime, he called 'Hello Darky' several times but got no reply. He became very exasperated and after calling 'Darky' again with the same result, he finally shouted into his

51

'Darky' again with the same result, he finally shouted into his microphone, "Hello Darky, Hello Darky, Hello Darky, where are you, you little black bastard ?"

Another incident occurred one night when we were again over Belgium returning from Berlin. Our position was somewhere near Liege and things were quiet, when predicted flak suddenly burst too close for comfort and rocked the aircraft but didn't damage it. My immediate reaction was to shove the nose down and put the aircraft into a steep dive, because the next burst would have been in the same area and would most certainly have 'got us'.

There was also another incident when the 'cookie' (4,000 lb. bomb) did a 'hang up' and the Bomb Aimer couldn't release it over the target. If this happened the practice was to look for an alternative target on the return journey and release it by hand.

We eventually saw a searchlight battery with three beams, so we made a bomb run and although the Bomb Aimer could not use his bomb site, he released it by hand, and as it dropped the light went out ; we could picture everybody running for shelter. It wasn't a bad attack because the bomb burst close to where the lights were operating.

There were many operations to Berlin between November 1943 and March 1944 which were carried out by all Lancaster Forces from Nos. 1 and 5 Groups ; other aircraft being deployed over occupied countries on some of those nights.

At the end of the Battle of Berlin our crew had flown on nine operations to the City ; three of them out of four nights at the end of January when we were in the air for twenty four hours out of ninety six.

It was also a period of changing situations ; you could be watching Alexanders Ragtime Band featuring Tyronne Power, Don Ameche, and Alice Fay in a cinema in Lincoln at eight o' clock one night and the next night at eight o' clock be over Berlin.

I think the following story sums up a Bomber Crew's chance of survival.

The Squadron was briefed for a raid during the Battle of Berlin ; take off to be at 6pm. The crews reported at the normal time before the raid but on this occasion take off was put back for two hours.

To fill the time in two other Lancaster pilots and myself cycled back in the blackout to the mess and played table tennis to fill time in before the revised take off time. We returned to the crew room only to be told it would be 12 o' clock midnight ; so we returned to the mess and continued our game again.

The Squadron finally got off the ground at midnight and we landed back after another harrowing raid at 6am.

As the crews came into the Interrogation Room our main question was " Is everybody back ? " If not the flare-path was left on for a time until news was received that missing aircraft had been forced to land elsewhere, or no further communication was received from them when the lights of the flare-path would be turned off.

No further news was received from the aircraft of my table tennis partners who had failed to return and as I cycled from the airfield to the mess the flare-path was turned off.

After I had breakfast I looked in the Ante room and there on the table were the bats and balls as we had left them before they flew off into Eternity (both were killed).

The Battle of Berlin which lasted from November 1943 to March 1944 cost Bomber Command over 500 aircraft and approximately 3,500 aircrew, either killed or taken prisoner.

I always made a practice when we reached the enemy coast on a return journey to put the nose of the aircraft down and dive steeply to about 2,000ft before levelling out and skating back over the North Sea. My Engineer always drew my attention to the fuel consumption during this practice but as long as we had sufficient to get us back, the cost in fuel was worth it.

This practice also brought me into a forecast which the staff of the Control Tower back at the airfield would make between themselves as to which aircraft would be the first back from a raid, ours or one piloted by 'Bunny Lee' an Australian pilot with roughly the same number of operations as our crew up to our being shot down and honours were about even.

I always thought that Bunny survived a tour of operations but at a recent Squadron reunion dinner I was told that he and his crew failed to return from their last operation.

There were other operations apart from those to Berlin during late 1943/44 and on looking at my log book the names of some of the towns or cities were Stuttgart, Augsburg, Munich, Leipzig, Stettin and Essen etc.

The operation to Stettin was made on the 5th January 1944 and took nine hours flying time, and even though it was in the middle of winter, the return journey over the North Sea was flown partly in daylight.

We were told at the briefing for the raid that dawn would break over the sea North of Holland, and it was a possibility the Germans would despatch fighters to intercept us, so it was necessary to fly as low as possible.

At daybreak, we had already been in the air for seven hours and were looking forward to landing, this was an incentive to drop as low as we could, and I flew the remainder of the trip at fifty feet above the waves until we reached the East Coast. No enemy action materialised.

Operation Leipzig 19th February 1944

Our crew flew on this operation which cost Bomber Command seventy eight aircraft.

It was another raid when the forecast winds were wrong, they were much stronger than expected and resulted in the bomber stream arriving over the target early.

The raid was made during the Battle of Berlin and as the two Cities are fairly close to each other the German Nightfighter Command expected another raid on Berlin, to which City we appeared to be heading, and for the first time I can remember Dornier bombers flew above the bomber stream on either side dropping flares to suspend in the air and form a 'lane' towards Berlin. They were also helpful to the nightfighters.

The turning point to fly south to Leipzig was ignored by several crews who for some unknown reason decided to take up the time by flying towards Berlin where they were caught in the 'lane' of flares which never seemed to go out and hung there for what seemed like ages. We saw all this happening as we flew towards Leipzig, I had decided to risk flying over the City and go round again on the East side by which time path finders would be dropping markers on zero hour. We could bomb on them and hopefully be away.

On the return journey we saw many combats but were not troubled ourselves.

In March 1944 there was talk of an invasion which many thought would come in the summer and we were called to a briefing one day for a raid different to all the others.

The raid was to be made against a factory making powered gliders for the Germans at a factory at Chateauroux in unoccupied France.

This attack was to be nothing like the high altitude bombing of German Cities; it was to be made by twenty two aircraft bombing individually between 7,000ft to approximately 11,000ft flying in full moonlight.

The raid would be controlled by a Master of Ceremonies flying a Lancaster who would open the attack by placing a red spot fire on top of a large hangar and then call in the attacking force with the first wave carrying 4,000lb and nine 500lb bombs. The first and last bomb fitted with delayed action fuses to explode several hours later.

The second wave of Bombers would carry incendiaries to set the factory alight.

We were to fly from our Base, another Squadron from Coningsby would also be on the raid and both Squadrons had to rendezvous at a cross-roads two miles north of the target which would be marked by a Master of Ceremonies five minutes before zero hour. The first wave of attackers were called Apples and the second wave Pears with the Master of Ceremonies called Big Stiff.

The met forecast was for cloud cover at fairly low level on route over France, clearing well north of the target to give us visibility to identify land marks such as rivers.

However the cloud cover extended a lot further south than Paris and we did not clear it until a few minutes before 'Big Stiff' was due to mark the cross-roads.

As E.T.A. approached we waited for him to call up, which he did on time saying he had found the rendezvous and would be dropping the marker.

We waited for him to do this because our E.T.A. had not come up with a corresponding identification of the cross-roads. To our relief when the marker dropped we were only three miles from it and by that time we were down to our bombing height - 7,200ft ; I commenced circling the cross-roads and could see the factory a couple of miles down the road. The planes continued to circle as the M.C. ordered ; and this gave the night shift at the factory sufficient time to evacuate before we commenced our attack.

The first aircraft bombed on time in perfect conditions without any opposition, except for one gun which was firing near the Town of Chateauxroux a few miles south. I was surprised when the first aircraft dropped its 4,000lb bomb on the airfield adjacent to the factory with the other bombs also bursting on the field. We were the second aircraft to attack and as the target was only 250 yards wide and half a mile long running by the side of a road, we came in on a diagonal run across it. It was perfect for the Bomb Aimer who could see where he had placed his bombs ; the 4,000lb bomb exploded on a workshop and destroyed it as

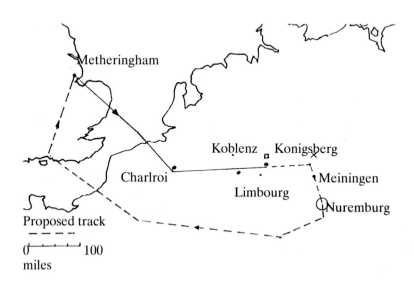

The planned route to bomb Nuremberg

55

the photograph proved, and the 500lb bombs straddled all the buildings ; it was a perfect bomb run.

After bombing we turned 180° and ran up the side of the road observing the result of the rest of the attack ; after the first wave had done their job the target looked gutted with smoke and flames, but the second wave went into fire it with their incendiaries.

One crew on the return journey talked continuously with their RT switched on, and although they were ordered to be quiet they kept on for some time.

One aircraft was lost on the raid and we wondered if it was the crew who 'broadcast'.

Many years after in the 1980's I visited Port o Pollensa in Majorca several times and made friends with quite a number of French people.

One lady in particular, who spoke English, was very friendly with my wife and I and on one occasion we were talking about the War. The French were evidently very appreciative of the R.A.F. ; I mentioned the Chateauxroux raid and the time given for the night shift to evacuate the factory before the attack commenced. There were a number of French people stood around and she turned to them and talked to them for about a minute.

I noticed their faces showed a look of appreciation at what she was saying because I was suddenly embraced, kissed on both cheeks and patted on the back ; our friend had told them about the raid which had given them great pleasure to hear and of the time given to workers to evacuate the factory, otherwise many would have been killed.

On one occasion In the Mess I was talking to our Flight Commander who had finished his second tour and was waiting for a posting, he was giving me his views on what would be happening on German night fighter aerodromes at that particular time as they were preparing for the nights operations.

I was later going to a briefing for the nights operation, and it was his usual way of testing your reaction to dangers you might meet.

At that time the Battle of Berlin was in full swing and he already knew the target, so my aim was to persuade him to divulge it ; would it be the Big City ? or I hoped, one where the defences were not as heavy and concentrated.

We were standing next to a rustic fireplace in the mess which was part of a large Nissen hut ; and he went on about the German defences getting better, as he did so he started scratching the mantelpiece with a pen knife.

At first I did not take much notice but when he scratched the letter 'S' followed by 'T' I began to take notice. Was he identifying the target ? if so, it certainly wasn't Berlin. All the time he was talking he was scratching letters, the ST was followed by UTTGART, STUTTGART - what a relief when he looked at me and nodded, it wasn't Berlin after all thank goodness but Southern Germany. The reason I am writing of this conversation is that ten years after the War I made a nostalgic visit to Metheringham ; and in the old mess which was partly in ruins with half the corrugated roof missing, stood the same fireplace, which had been protected from the weather by the roof, part of which covered it. At the time I remembered the conversation with the Flight Commander and his spelling out of the target on the mantelpiece with a knife.

Naturally I looked to see if there was any evidence of his work, and there were the same letters which were in the brickwork after all those years - remarkable.

A few weeks before we were shot down I was told that a mine laying operation was planned during the April moon period and our crew would be involved.

Mines were to be laid around the Gdynia canal on the far side of the Baltic, and three or four aircraft from 106 Squadron would fly at low level to drop the mines.

Anti aircraft fire was expected and would probably be firing at us horizontally.

We practised for the operation by flying low level exercises around the central part of England.

However before our crew could participate in the raid we were shot down on the way to Nuremberg, but at a Squadron Reunion dinner in 1997 I met an ex Flight Engineer from a crew who operated about the same time as ours, who told me they had taken our place and the operation was a success.

It was a long flight mostly low level apart from over Denmark where they had to gain height, before descending over the Baltic and running into the drop zone at 100ft with heavy flak to contend with ; they all returned having successfully laid the mines.

Reference must be made to two anti aircraft weapons met during the winter of 1943/44.

One was named 'Scarecrew' and the other was a rocket which flew horizontally at a certain height and changed course, then increased speed by further propulsion, like a meteor.

The scarecrew would be put up by the Germans usually in a dark part of the sky on the route where no other defence was in use. The idea was to scare aircrew because it would suddenly burst and resemble an aircraft being hit, bursting into flames, exploding and bits descending to the ground. The only difference was that an aircraft plunging down in flames and exploding would hit the ground and splash along it whereas the scarecrew would burn out and never reach the ground.

There is some controversy about whether scarecrews existed, but I can say, without any doubt, in my mind they did.

The rocket projectile did not cause much trouble apart from keeping an eye on it until it burnt out ; as you watched it change course and regain speed with a burst from its tail it looked dangerous but I never saw one collide with an aircraft.

As heavy raids continued the night fighters took an increasing toll of Bombers, and they were guided on to their targets by radar operators on the ground.

This was countered by German speaking radio operators in England instructing the night fighter pilots to cancel the previous order and fly elsewhere.

In turn the Germans got over this by using coded music to let their pilots know the intended target. For instance marches were played if the target was Berlin and on many occasions I remember my Wireless Operator saying they were playing nothing but marches on the German radio.

To continue with the Battle of Berlin, on one of the operations our 4,000lb cookie exploded near the Reichstag ; this was confirmed by the photo of the burst which must have damaged the building.

Although we were losing a lot of bombers on the Berlin operations, aircrew were alerted to the possibility of German suicide troops landing in the vicinity of airfields to kill them on the ground and plans were ready to disperse crews away from their quarters to other sites on the airfield. At the time we thought the Germans must have been desperate to mount such an operation but maybe our raids were inflicting unacceptable damage to property and morale. However the attacks never materialised but our losses continued to rise.

Recently, and as a matter of interest I was looking at 'A Lancaster at War' Book and one of the photographs showed W/C Gibson, who was Commanding Officer of 106 Squadron before forming 617 Squadron for the dams raid, and several members of the Squadron in front of his Lancaster before he left. On looking through my log book and checking the serial No. of that aircraft found I flew it on several occasions when I joined the Squadron.

Our ground crew at Metheringham who looked after 'Q' for Queenie were of the best. They did their job magnificently and nothing was too much trouble.

I remember asking them if they could find a leather cushion for the pilot's position and the next time I flew it was in place ; I think they took it from the Flight Commander's aircraft (Note reference to this later in the book).

They also named the aircraft 'QUEEN OF SHEBA' and painted a picture of a nude lady just under the pilot's window.

When we returned from an operation the crew shot a line to them saying the flak over the target was so hot she came back tanned.

We had a drink with them once a week at the local village pub when operations permitted ; I remember one of the lads came from Leeds and another from Liverpool.

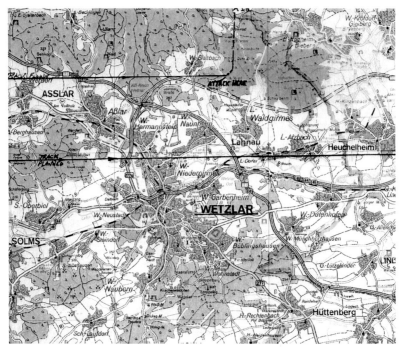

Map of Wetzlar area showing position of Nightfighter attack on 30/31st March 43 and subsequent course of "Q" Queenie before crashing.

After I was repatriated from Germany at the end of the War the R.A.F. sent me on a refresher course flying Oxfords at Coleby Grange near Lincoln.

I was waiting in the bus station at Lincoln for a bus to the airfield one night when a voice shouted "Dick" and on turning saw one of them running towards me. The last time I saw him was at dispersal on the night we were shot down and as he shook my hand he said "All the ground crew had been relieved and happy when they heard I had survived, but were grieved over the other lads who lost their lives".

Before I leave this part of the story on our operation experiences I will relate what happened on a raid to Augsburg in February 1944 when the main target was the Daimler Benz factory where engines were assembled for Messerschmidt aircraft. It was the first time an operation was planned with two waves of aircraft bombing two hours apart.

We were in the first wave and the weather over Germany was clear with a starlit sky, no cloud and snow on the ground. It was our second visit to Bavaria, having bombed Munich on a previous operation ; and as you gained experience it was possible to identify cities by the position of searchlights and anti aircraft guns. Augsburg and Munich are both in searchlights and anti aircraft guns. Augsburg and Munich are both in Bavaria and as we flew east towards them both defences were in action, especially the searchlights.

We identified one cluster of searchlights ahead of us as 'Augsburg' and confirmed with the Navigator's H²s that this was the target. However as we approached the two minutes before zero hour when markers were dropped by the Path Finder Force nothing happened which was strange ; a point I conveyed to the crew.

The Mid Upper Gunner immediately came on the R.T. and said the markers were being dropped on the beam of the port side.

I looked over my left shoulder and there they were dropping on the other city which of course was Augsburg ; we had mistakenly identified Munich for Augsburg. I turned towards the target which was several minutes flying away and knew we should be over the City when the first wave were already on the return journey.

I thought about all the defences concentrating on one aircraft - ours - at the same time we would be on our own on enemy radar. Should we drop the bombs straight away and skirt the City to get on the return track or risk it and bomb the fires in the City which were now well alight.

I decided to carry out the operation and approached the target. Fortunately the flak was not very accurate although some of it too close for comfort ; I managed to evade the searchlights and the Bomb Aimer dropped the bombs from our solitary aircraft twenty minutes after the Main Force had gone.

It was an uncomfortable few minutes as we flew over the City and were relieved to get to the other side.

Nuremberg 30th / 31st March 1944

The day before Nuremberg Bomber Command was set for a raid on Brunswick.

Four crews were on the last ten trips of their tours and it looked as though they would complete the thirty operations (a complete tour) at about the same time, so it was decided to stagger the remaining trips. Following this decision we were to stand down for the Brunswick raid. My crew were keen to do a second tour of twenty trips with 617 Squadron who were stationed a few miles away at Woodhall Spa ; as mentioned before this station, Metheringham and Coningsby formed a Base and there would have been no difficulty with the transfer.

However the operation to Brunswick was cancelled because the Met Forecast was not good.

On the 30th March Nuremberg was the target and I was told by the Flight Commander my crew would be stood down again. I informed the lads of the orders but as one man said ; that as we had been a stand down crew for a cancelled operation one of the other crews should do so for the Nuremberg raid ; and asked me to see the Flight Commander again.

Although I had to decide whether or not to let the order stand I agreed that we should be put on the Battle Order and gave my views to the Flight Commander.

At first he said the order would not be reversed but after some thought to our request changed his decision. It was our last trip.

With only three weeks to go to the end of our tour (the raid was to be the crew's 22nd trip) I remember that after the afternoon briefing, some of the crews had reservations about the operation.

The attack was planned for what would normally have been the middle of the stand down period, when a near full moon would be visible.

The forecast was for high cloud on the outward route with the target clear.

However in the early afternoon a reconnaissance aircraft reported that the route would be clear of cloud but the target would probably be covered. This was after the crews had been briefed for the operation, but it was not cancelled.

We took off in Lancaster ND 535 'Q' and climbed on course over the Norfolk Coast towards Belgium. The moon was bright and almost full, making near daylight conditions.

At our cruising height of 21,000ft the air temperature was very low and the Bomber stream began to make condensation trails as we flew on route, over Belgium towards the long leg which ran from South of the Ruhr East to a turning point North West of Nuremberg. It was this long leg that crews were apprehensive about because it ran for over two hundred miles.

We did not know at the time that the route took us over two night fighter beacons ; and the German Controller, ignoring diversionary operations over Germany and the North Sea, transferred most of his fighter force to those beacons to await the Bombers.

Flying conditions over Germany were ideal for fighter aircraft against slow bombers who had inferior armament ; and the sky was absolutely clear with a near full moon and four-engined bombers making condensation trails which could be seen for miles.

The fighters began their attack, and from the number of tracers being fired, it appeared there were combats everywhere ; I saw around thirty aircraft go down in a short period and as we continued to the target the ground became covered with burning aircraft.

We continuously operated the 'banking search' looking for enemy aircraft coming up from below. This was achieved by turning steeply to port for 15º to see if fighters were preparing to attack and then banking to return to the original course.

I made reference to Monica on the Leipzig raid which was a much more reliable aircraft detector with its audio system than Fishpond (visual aid) attached to H²s which more often than not failed to work, as ours did on the Nuremberg raid.

YEAR 1944		AIRCRAFT		PILOT, OR 1ST PILOT	2ND PILOT, PUPIL OR PASSENGER	DUTY (INCLUDING RESULTS AND REMARKS)
MONTH	DATE	Type	No.			
—	—	—	—	—	—	TOTALS BROUGHT FORWARD
FEB.	24	LANCASTER	ND 535	SELF	CREW	SCHWEINFURT INCENDIARIES
—	25	—	—	—	—	AUGSBURG "
					FEBRUARY	LANCASTER
			S/LDR. F/comm 106 SQDN		106 SQDN	
					1.3.44	
			W/comm 106 SQDN		R Baxter P/o	
MAR	1	LANCASTER	ND 535	SELF	CREW	N. F. T.
—	3	—	—	—	—	H. L B.
—	7	—	—	—	—	X COUNTRY & BOMBING
—	7	—	JB 601	—	—	NIGHT BOMBING
—	9	—	ND 535	—	—	R.T. TEST
—	10	—	—	—	—	CHATEAUROUX (4,500 FT. 11000LB & 1000LBS) (AIRCRAFT FACTORY)
—	1	—	—	—	—	STUTTGART 4000 LB & INCENDIARY
—	12	—	—	—	—	AIR TO SEA FIRING
—	24	—	—	—	—	BERLIN LANDED WING 14000 LB INCENDIARY
—	25	—	—	—	—	FROM WING
—	26	—	—	—	—	ESSEN 4000LB & INCENDIARIES
	29		JB 641		—	AIR TEST
	30	LANCASTER	ND 535	SELF	CREW	Operation Nuremburg
				RETURNED TO ENGLAND 29.5.45		

GRAND TOTAL [Cols. (1) to (10)]

.................Hrs.................Mins.

TOTALS CARRIED FORWARD

Last entry in my log book "Failed to Return"

SINGLE-ENGINE AIRCRAFT				MULTI-ENGINE AIRCRAFT						PASS-ENGER	INSTR/CLOUD FLYING [incl. in cols. (1) to (10)]	
DAY		NIGHT		DAY			NIGHT					
DUAL	PILOT	DUAL	PILOT	DUAL	1ST PILOT	2ND PILOT	DUAL	1ST PILOT	2ND PILOT		DUAL	PILOT
(1)	(2)	(3)	(4)	(5)	(6)	(7)	(8)	(9)	(10)	(11)	(12)	(13)
43·10	53·05	4·15		102·00	185·50	5·30	26·35	156·20	5·20	38·45	48·35	24·45
								7·40				
								8·00				
					12·30			35·25				
					·40							
					·50							
					2·45							
								1·15				
					·50							
6·7 & 50 sagns								5·20				
								7·25				
					1·00			7·20				
					·30							
								4·45				
Failed To Return												
				W/C. Commanding,								
				No. 106 Squadron.								
(1)	(2)	(3)	(4)	(5)	(6)	(7)	(8)	(9)	(10)	(11)	(12)	(13)

We had been flying the long leg for many miles and when we were in a position sixty miles north west of Nuremberg our luck changed ; a fighter attacked with tracer and cannon fire which hit the port mainplane and outer engine, flashed past outside the perspex covering of the cockpit and between my legs. I remembered when we were attacked north of Frankfurt in December and prayed we would not go up in flames. However within three or four seconds the port outer engine and mainplane were alight.

It was always the one you didn't see that shot you down as in our case and if Monica had been available we would have been aware of the fighters approach.

There was only one action to take - I gave the order to abandon aircraft. The Engineer feathered the port engine as he helped me with the controls because we were going down at a very fast rate ; and the next few seconds I remember vividly.

The Bomb Aimer acknowledged my order to bail out and said he was leaving the aircraft. The Navigator came to the cockpit to escape through the front hatch. The Rear Gunner also acknowledged the order but said he could not get out of his turret ; this was because the port outer engine powered the turret ; the alternative way was to turn the turret by hand controls in order to fall out backwards. There was no reply from the Mid Upper Gunner and the Wireless Operator, I assumed they must have been killed by the burst of fire which ran along the side of the aircraft.

The Flight Engineer handed me a parachute from one of two in the rack at his side. I managed to connect one of the hooks on the chute to the harness I was wearing, (we did not wear seat type chutes) at the same time trying to control a blazing aircraft which was diving at well over 300mph. I gave up all hope of survival and waited for the impact ; a terrifying experience.

That is the last thing I remember because the aircraft exploded with a full bomb load (we had no time to jettison) and 1,500 gallons of high octane fuel, which must have ignited and caused the explosion.

As I lost consciousness I did have a feeling of being lifted out of the cockpit and must have been propelled through the perspex canopy.

When the petrol tanks exploded in the port wing outside my window a fire ball must have been created in the aircraft which would incinerate anything in its path, and I must have been just ahead of it as I was blown from the aircraft.

Many years later I was told an unopened parachute was found next to the body of the flight Engineer who had landed in a wood 6 kilometres from the wreckage of the aircraft. He must have been blown out like me, but I was lucky my parachute had opened probably by the force of the explosion ; also as he could have taken the parachutes out of the rack in any order I might have had the one that didn't open. There is also the possibility that he was unconscious or killed by the explosion, but as we were only two feet apart in the cockpit when the aircraft went up, and I did not operate my parachute, because I was unconscious ; something did, I was extremely lucky.

When I regained consciousness and realised what had happened my first thought was " where am I ? " ; then I heard the sound of aircraft engines as the main force passed overhead, and I was suspended somewhere over Germany by parachute.

I expected to feel the parachute supports in front of my face but could not find them - I thought I was coming down without a parachute !.

I desperately groped around and located the one hook attachment and hung on, this attachment was well above my head, evidently the pad of the parachute once it has opened rises up to a position over your head and I wasn't aware of this.

By this time I did not know how quickly I was descending, I was coming down without flying boots and as I looked up saw the canopy of the parachute quite clearly in the bright moonlight, riddled in parts with a number of burnt small holes, some half an inch in diameter ; and it was terrifying because I was afraid that my descent might be too fast for a safe landing.

Although the moon was bright I could not see the ground, but there were several fires burning which I took to be from our aircraft. The fires did not help me to judge my altitude because I did not know the size of them.

I also had facial injuries including a nose bleed, these must have occurred when I was blown out of the aircraft.

As my thoughts dwelt on landing, I hit the ground with an almighty wallop and rolled backwards down a small hill. When I reached the bottom I regained my wind and could see hills silhouetted against the night sky.

My neck and back were very painful and when I attempted to stand, my right leg collapsed. It was out of line just above the ankle and I knew it was broken. I must have then lost consciousness again and when I came to the moon was low in the sky behind the hills. I could not walk and waited for someone to arrive.

I soon heard shouting in German and realised I had left Metheringham an hour and a half to two hours before where everyone spoke English and here I was for the first time listening to a German voice.

I saw a torch light about two hundred yards away so I shouted back and the torch came towards me. A number of people arrived and the torch was shone in my face.

I could make out both young and elderly men ; one of the younger men started shouting and was about to hit me in the face with a rifle when he was stopped by one of the older men. One or two of them went off to search the wreckage and the others wrapped me in the parachute placed me on a stretcher and carried me to a horse drawn cart which took me to a small village called Konigsberg about one thousand metres away.

When we arrived I was carried up some steps on the outside of a building and placed on the floor of what was the Bergemeister's Office.

After the War I was informed the German Pilot who shot us down was O/Lt Martin Becker their night Fighter Ace who received a very high decoration when he was sent for by Adolf Hitler the day after the raid, having been credited with eight victims on the night.

I was also told that he shot down over fifty allied aircraft during the bombing of Germany and was one of their night fighter aces.

There have been several reasons put forward for the unacceptable loss of 97 Bombers and their Aircrew. One of them is 'They knew we were coming' ; the other one is the weather, not bad weather but clear weather and temperatures so low they created condensation trails.

As one who participated in the raid I accept the latter reason ; and as the route happened to pass over two night fighter beacons, it made it easier for their pilots to get amongst us and shoot us down with their armament, 20mm and •50 calibre cannon and machine guns compared to our pea shooters •303 calibre machine guns.

What grieves me even after fifty years, is why we were allowed to go. The weather reports on the day of the raid which were obtained by P.R.U. aircraft changed from one which would give some protection to the bombers to a later one which completely changed the picture and should have influenced a decision to call it off.

Hauptman Martin Becker
Luftwaffe Nightfighter Ace who
shot down 'Q' Queenie and seven
other bombers on Nuremberg Raid

Chapter 7

Prisoner of war

Starting from the time I was carried up the stairs at the Burgermeister's Office after being shot down and badly wounded, I arrived in the village at approximately 2am on the 31st March 1944 and as mentioned before was laid on a stretcher (lattice type) and put on the floor with a local resident detailed to watch me by the local policeman ; this man had been invalided out of the German Army after being wounded on the Eastern front where he lost an arm.

By this time I was in a lot of pain and wondering when I would receive medical attention. As the day passed so the pain increased in my ankles neck and back ; and I appeared to be the object of much interest for the local inhabitants who came to the Police Station with their families, especially children, to look at the R.A.F. pilot who had suddenly dropped from the skies.

The ladies must have expected to see a rough customer because the German propaganda machine described R.A.F. aircrew ' Luft Gangsters' whereas what they saw was a young man in shock and severely wounded who was waiting for medical attention.

Strangely although I was the enemy it seemed to bring out the motherly instinct in the ladies because they clucked their tongues, shook their heads and even had a sympathetic look in their eyes.

The local people must have come from miles around the village because when I saw it in daylight it was just a hamlet with probably no more than a hundred people living there.

Sometime in the afternoon I heard a motorcycle arrive outside the building and a minute or so later the local doctor entered the room.

William Schupp who guarded me in Burgermeisters office after I was shot down
Died 9.2.99

As soon as he saw me lying there he started yelling at me which I could stand, but then he got hold of both my feet and started shaking them about ; as I have already mentioned one of my legs above the ankle was out of line by about 30º.

I screamed out because the pain was excruciating ; whereupon he left the room still shouting and I heard him drive away.

I was in absolute agony by this time and the guard was showing concern about my injuries.

I visited Konigsberg in June 1997, but more of that later on, when I was informed that the doctor was a fanatical Nazi, who soon after he saw me was drafted into the army, sent to the Russian Front and was killed.

After my experience with the Doctor I had given up hope of medical treatment, thinking that he would not order my removal to a hospital, but let me suffer until I was in the hands of the Luftwaffe as a prisoner of War under the Geneva Convention.

During the afternoon a young boy about ten years of age came into the Police Station and said in broken English " Me English Tutor". I thought it improbable that he would teach English at that age, and after several minutes trying to understand him, I realised he had an English tutor, and asked him to bring him to me.

About half an hour later an elderly gentleman came into the Station and said in English that he was the boy's Tutor. He then described having seen my aircraft spiralling down in flames and what a terrible spectacle it had been as it crashed and exploded with all the bombs still on board. For several minutes he could not stop talking about it but I was finally able to interrupt his account which certainly had affected him.

I asked him if he would enquire of the Police Officer if I would be taken to hospital because I was in severe pain, and he was told that I would be transferred later in the day.

At about 6pm after several more local people had visited me I was taken by stretcher down the Station steps and put on a horse drawn cart escorted by the gentleman with one arm, and the driver.

It was the first time I had seen the village in daylight and noticed it was built on the side of a steep hill.

We set off up the road and after travelling a quarter of a mile the escort pointed in the direction of a large wood 1000 yds away which had areas of smoke emitting from it. I was told it was from the aircraft when it crashed and exploded. He then pointed to some more smoke which rose from a spot over the brow of a hill in open countryside, evidently it was the site of the crash.

The Lancaster had certainly made a mess of the wood and no doubt the same to the field where it crashed and exploded.

Some fifty years later when I made the visit I was taken to the crash site by Herr Lepper who was fourteen years of age in 1944 and carried the torch by which they found me near the wreckage.

He said the aircraft had made a hole in the field approximately 17 yards across and 6 yards deep and even now there is a slight depression in the ground where it was filled in. On the visit I found a piece of red perspex on site about 1½ inches long and ½ inch wide with a hole pierced down the centre.

Reference is made to this piece of perspex in the opening chapters of the book and we have identified it as a switch cover from the 'G' set which Jonathan had noticed on a coloured video of a Lancaster's navigation system.

To go back to my conveyance from Konigsberg in 1944, although I was in pain I observed the beautiful countryside with rolling wooded hills and undulating areas of agricultural land, all on what seemed to be high country which stretched for several miles in every direction.

I did not know my destination, and hoped it would not take long to get there. Our progress was slow and the wheels crunched on the rough road as they slowly turned.

After about three miles we started to descend from the high country and continued our slow journey for an indeterminable time, until houses came into view as we approached a town.

The town stands on a river it is called Wetzlar. I visited this City in 1997 which is very picturesque and has a fine Cathedral together with many old buildings.

We stopped at a building near the river and turned into the grounds, which had been a school but was then a Lazarett for German soldiers wounded on the Russian Front.

On the visit last year we were directed to the site of the building which had been a school before and after the war and had only been demolished eighteen months previously to make way for a bank.

I was taken on the stretcher from the cart into the hospital and put in a room where I was the sole occupant. My escort left me after I thanked him which he understood (to come back to my visit last year I enquired about this man because I wanted to thank him again, but was told he was now eighty years old, had Alzeimers Disease and could no longer communicate).

After I was put into a bed, several minutes later three doctors arrived and examined my injuries. They told me I would be going to the operating theatre for treatment and then proceeded to ask me about Winston Churchill as to what kind of a man he was.

I thought this rather strange because the War was in its fifth year and they should have known all about him. It could have been that they did not believe Germany would win the War and because they could not say so were trying to find some basis for thinking the Allies would not punish the German people.

However their attitude toward me was entirely opposite to the Nazi doctor who had ranted and raved at me and more or less tortured me when he aggravated my wounds.

I was taken to the Operating Theatre, put under anaesthetic and when I regained consciousness, my right leg and ankle had been set and plastered, a small piece of metal taken from my ankle, and the left leg and foot was heavily bandaged. My neck was X rayed and I was told that it was not broken but it was badly jarred, and would probably trouble me in later years, which it has.

I was in the Lazarett for a further twenty four hours and during that time several young German soldiers who were patients, brought me books, whilst others were just curious to see an R.A.F. Pilot. I have to say most of them were about my age and with all of us wearing pyjamas we could have been on the same side.

These young soldiers who were from the Eastern front, must have seen terrible battles between Russian and German Forces and most of them would have made up their minds that Germany had already lost the War, because they were taking severe punishment on the Russian Front.

I often wonder how many of these boys survived the War, because when they were fit they would have gone back to the East.

At the end of twenty four hours I was moved from the Lazarett by a horse drawn cart to a Luftwaffe Night Fighter Station, where I joined eight other R.A.F. Aircrew who had been shot down on the Nuremberg Raid.

I was the only injured airman and as we were put in cells, the Commander of the Station who was immaculately dressed in a uniform of superb quality warned us there would be severe punishment if any attempt was made to escape. In my case this was impossible because I could not move without assistance and he told the other members of the party to assist me if I wanted to use the toilet, and gave instructions that I should be made as comfortable as possible.

When he left we had our first chance to communicate with each other but only in whispers in case the Luftwaffe personnel heard us. There was no doubt from everyone's opinion about the raid, that Bomber Command had been severely hit by Night Fighters and had lost many aircraft, a figure I was not to know until the interrogation at Dulag Luft. One of our party, a Sergeant Air Gunner, had parachuted from his aircraft to land on the airfield, and then attempted to damage aircraft on the ground. He was lucky not to be severely punished but evidently for him he thought the War was not over until he had caused damage to aircraft on the ground.

The next morning we were transported to Geissan Station for the journey to Dulag Luft Interrogation Centre at Oberhausel near Frankfurt. I had to be carried every time we were moved but we finally settled at the station to await the train. There were many people in uniform because Geissan appeared to be a mainline station and as I looked around at all types of uniforms, i.e. Gestapo (black) Army (green) Luftwaffe (blue) and Stormtroopers (khaki) with Nazi

70

armband, I realised that England in a sense was very far away and Germany was a sinister and evil Country, which made our future very uncertain. I think it was the sight of nearly everyone in uniform, (only seen on the cinema screens) which conveyed in a way, a state of severe depression.

As we waited for the train I noticed one man in a khaki uniform with a swastika armband looking at us with hate and murder in his eyes. He suddenly dashed toward us and smashed an Australian in our group in the face with a massive fist and knocked him to the ground. The Aussie was shocked for a split second then made to take retaliatory action but quickly realised that all of us might be killed because the accompanying guard could not, if he wanted to, stop the German from probably shooting us ; no doubt helped by some of the other German Servicemen. It was a very dangerous situation but thank goodness the Aussie realised it.

All of us were relieved when the train arrived, with cattle trucks attached to the back for our conveyance. As we travelled with the doors opened we continuously saw wreckages of R.A.F. Bombers on either side, and we then knew that the losses on the Nuremberg Raid must have been horrific.

Chapter 8

Dulag Luft

The journey to Dulag Luft was very depressing and I was in a lot of pain from the injuries to my neck, back and ankle. The Luftwaffe guards certainly made the most of our misfortune by gloating over the number of wrecked Bombers on route.

We finally arrived at Oberhausel, the train having been delayed by a number of stoppages due to damage to the lines caused by Allied bombing, this uplifted our morale a little.

I remember the Dulag Luft complex was a combination of buildings where prisoners were locked in small cells approximately eight feet by four feet, with a bed. If a visit to the toilet was required you had to operate an indicator at the side of the door which dropped a wooden arm on the wall in the corridor, you then had to wait until a guard saw it, whereupon he would unlock the cell door for you to make the visit. Again I had to be helped by another prisoner if I wanted to go the toilet.

The main purpose at Dulag Luft was to give you an intensive interrogation by Luftwaffe Intelligence Officers using every kind of trick to get you to talk.

Before this interrogation however you were locked in the cell for a few days when life was made very uncomfortable, not only by the size of the cell but also a practice used by the Germans at night. This was to increase the heat in the cell to a very high level to make the occupant sweat profusely and suffer sleeplessness. The heating apparatus was

International Red Cross Committee
Geneva. Switzerland

ARRIVAL REPORT FORM

Date:
Name: Surname: Service Number:
Rank:
Trade:
R.A.F., R.C.A.F., R.A.A.F., R.N.Z.A.F., S.A.A.F., U.S.A.A.F.,
U.S.N.A.F., F.A.A.
Date of birth:
Where born:
Profession:
Religion:
Married:
How many children:
Home address:
Next of kin:
What was your payment during the war:
When shot down:
Where shot down:
By:
Where taken prisoner:
By:
Squadron: Group: Command:
Station: Station No:
Letters and number of aircraft:
Type of aircraft:
How is your health: Wounded:

Members of the crew
Name: Surname: Number: Wounded: Killed: P.O.W:

Date. Signature.

Bogus Red Cross form

72

somehow built into the wall and you couldn't do anything about it except to shout to the guards to turn the heating down which, of course, they ignored.

After the War I read a book on War atrocities by the Germans and although the 'heat treatment' at Dulag Luft was a minor part of their programme, it was never the less recognised by the Allies as inhuman.

Whilst at Dulag Luft a Luftwaffe Medical Orderly came each day to look at the plaster and bandages on my legs. I was not receiving treatment to my neck which was stiff and prevented me from turning or raising my head.

After the third day I noticed a black substance seeping through the plastercast on my right foot and knew something was wrong - I had received frostbite to my foot when parachuting to the ground and although this had been treated the plaster cast was placed over the foot ; it was at this spot from which the black substance came.

I pointed this out to the Medical Orderly when he came but he just looked at it and left the cell.

The next day a different Orderly came, who was Austrian, and spoke a little English. He noticed the discharge straight away and said I would have to go to hospital, but unfortunately the hospital used when it was necessary to take prisoners for treatment, had been damaged by bombs and he would have to try and have me admitted elsewhere. He then told me that if the foot was not treated gangrene may set in.

Later in the day my cell door was opened and I was again carried to a horse drawn cart and taken to a building in its own grounds nearby which looked escape proof. This was because the building was a mental institution which was obvious by the activities of patients I saw in the grounds. I think I am right in remembering that it was the practice of the Nazi regime to eliminate mentally retarded people, if so some of the inmates I saw would not have long to live.

I was met at the main door by a chap with a Welsh accent, who hoisted me on his back fireman fashion and carried me up several flights of steps to an attic type room at the top where he put me down on one of two beds. He was very inquisitive about what had happened to me

Caterpillar Club Membership

73

and naturally I was suspicious because I thought the Germans were using him to obtain information which I would not divulge to them. However he was a legitimate member of the British Army, serving with the Paratroops Regiment, and had been captured during ground action against the Germans in the Middle East.

I was expecting to see an Interrogation Officer but after being in captivity for three days, realised isolating me was part of the 'softening up' procedure before interrogation.

Midway through the afternoon the door opened and a German Luftwaffe Officer entered. He introduced himself as a Ober /Lieut. and immediately assumed a friendly attitude, calling me by name which surprised me as I had not given the Germans full information of my name rank and number.

He said he had lived in Kent for a few years and talked about certain features of that County and London. I was of the opinion that he had never been to Kent but done his homework to learn something of the County. He said he was sorry I had been shot down but it would be helpful to my family and me if I filled in the 'Red Cross Form' which he presented to me, so they could notify them that I was safe. I read through the document and noticed there were several questions which did not come within the requirements of the Geneva Convention, apart from name, rank and number. These questions were :

(1)   Name
(2)   Rank
(3)   Squadron and Group
(4)   Type of aircraft
(5)   Station
(6)   Letter and No. of aircraft
(7)   Names of crew

I decided to name the members of my crew because I knew five of them were killed and their relatives would have to wait six months before being notified of their deaths (in that time they would be reported missing), whereas if I gave their numbers it could be that the Germans would notify the Red Cross of their deaths immediately and save their families six months of worry and distress.

The other member of my crew Wally Paris, the Bomb Aimer, had escaped from the aircraft before it exploded and was probably alive so I omitted his name from the form.

When I had written the necessary information I handed the form back to the Luftwaffe Officer who scanned through it and gave it back to me, saying that I had not completed it and this would only delay notification of my safety to my family.

I told him I had submitted information required only under the Geneva Convention and the questions I had not answered were not required to be given by a Prisoner of War.

He informed me that I would be visited and interrogated by a member of the Security Branch, hinting it might be the Gestapo, and they would require all questions on the form to be answered, otherwise my survival might not be notified to the Red Cross because they would not treat me as a Prisoner of War.

After he left the room, it made me realise my position was very precarious at the least, because any future interrogator, from whatever service, would have my safety in his hands ; if it was the Gestapo he would probably treat me as a 'Terror Fleuger' as we were known, and transfer me to a Concentration Camp.

My eyes were fixed on the door for the remainder of the afternoon, wondering if the next time it was opened it would be by someone in a black uniform.

It did eventually open, not by the Gestapo, but by another Luftwaffe Officer, this time a major immaculately dressed and perfumed.

He strode up to me and ordered me in no uncertain manner to complete the Red Cross Forms and threw them on the bed. I have to say that at this point of my capture I was still in shock, with injuries giving me a lot of pain, and it would have been easy for me to give him the information.

His attitude was one of intimidation and for several seconds we stared at each other with him asking me questions and talking about things which if I had contradicted or confirmed would probably have completed the whole picture of the Squadron.

He then asked me questions about Navigational Aids, especially H²s which we had installed in our aircraft. This was a machine with a small round screen, operated by the Navigator and Wireless Operator ; it worked by sending signals to the ground from a scanner housed under the Lancaster, these were reflected back to the screen in the shape of the target to which the signals were aimed.

We had been told the Germans had recovered an H²s machine from an R.A.F. Bomber which had crashed and this Interrogator was trying to extract information so he could to tie up their records.

I told him I had never seen H²s but he said he knew our Squadron was using them, and followed this up by telling me about an H²s they had in their possession, no doubt this was the one mentioned earlier.

He then surprised me by asking out of the blue about two of the pilots on the Squadron, naming them as O'Leary and Hinkley. These two, Jack and Reg, were friends of mine and we slept in the same Nissen Hut. He then proceeded to name the Squadron 106 but wanted to know where it was located. At this point I was wondering just how much he did know, he had thrown the information at me and then quickly asked the Squadron whereabouts thinking I might be off guard. I resisted and he proceeded to name the Squadron Commander ; Wing Commander Baxter ; at last I knew his information was out of date but only just, because W/C Baxter had only recently left the Squadron and we had a new C.O.

He then told me that if I would not tell him where the Squadron was located he would gladly give me the information, and asked me if the name began with 'M' and finished with 'M', I knew then that he had in his files a considerable amount of data because we were stationed at Metheringham - beginning with M and ending with M.

He continued by telling me that ninety seven Bombers were lost on the Nuremberg Raid, and as the German Night Fighter Controller knew the target of the Bombers before they left England, he could have deployed all his day and night fighters to shoot down many more. I had observed many Bombers going down before we got our packet and although we had never lost over ninety Bombers before I knew his information was probably near the mark.

After all we had lost seventy four aircraft on a raid to Berlin seven days previously and thirty three on Essen two days after, so if the figure of ninety seven was correct Bomber Command lost two hundred and four aircraft within seven days with one thousand four hundred and forty aircrew missing. That would be the equivalent of ten Squadrons.

The interrogator said although I had not been co-operative he would give me further evidence of their intelligence capabilities and to my amazement produced a photograph of my aircraft in dispersal at Metheringham.

He concluded by saying they had all the information required on our Squadron, and if anything he knew more about it than I did. Whereupon he left.

After he had gone I thought about the photographs and realised it might not have been as hard to obtain as I first thought.

At the time I was shot down a 'Fido system' was being installed at Metheringham, this was to disperse fog to enable aircraft to land at night. Many workmen employed on this scheme were from Southern Ireland, which was neutral, and they had access to all corners of the airfield. It could have been that the photograph was taken by one of them and passed on to a German Agent.

At this point I must state that during the War many Southern Irishmen volunteered for Service with the British Forces fighting Germany. One of these became a friend of mine during training in Canada. His name was Moroney, naturally we called him Paddy, and although we separated when returning to England he also went on to fly Lancasters and was lost on a raid.

I understand the last message he sent from his damaged Bomber returning over the North Sea was that the aircraft was going down. No trace was ever found of the aircraft or crew, but he was one Irishman who recognised Germany as the enemy.

Chapter 9

Prisoner of war hospitals Obermassfeld and Meiningen

It was now time for me to be transferred to a recognised Prisoner of War Hospital for further treatment, so I, together with other injured aircrew, was put on a train at Oberhausel (Station for Dulag Luft) accompanied by two elderly Luftwaffe guards and travelled to Obermassfeld which was a journey of approximately five hours.

Obermassfeld is situated in a beautiful valley not far from Meiningen in Central Germany, after the War it became part of Eastern Germany.

I remember it as a village which could have come out of a children's story book, with Pinocchio as the main character. All the buildings were quaintly historic and there was a narrow hump backed bridge spanning a stream at the end of the village which completed the children's book image.

The hospital was a converted agricultural school, three storeys high, where you entered a courtyard which was enclosed on three sides by the building.

The medical staff were Prisoners of War and included a whole New Zealand Dental Unit captured in the Middle East (my American friend Bill who I had left at the mental hospital would have received expert treatment in their hands).

I was carried up three flights of stairs to a long room with double bunks occupied by injured or sick POW's. Most were American R.A.F. and Dominion Officers with the majority of them amputation cases and others like myself with fractured bones, including broken necks and backs.

The other patients were Army Officers who were seriously ill (e.g. Pneumonia, T.B.) and had been POW's as early as 1940 having been taken in France. Some of these were awaiting repatriation including a Peer, I forget his title but he was a Lord, the only heir to the family's estate and had been a POW since 1940, he was suffering from a serious chest ailment.

One of the occupants of the next double bunk was a captain in a Yorkshire Infantry Regiment who had been a steeplechase jockey before the War and had ridden a horse to third place in the Scottish Grand National. I believe he became a race horse trainer after the War.

My ankle was reset at Obermassfeld and again put in plaster, I was provided with a pair of crutches but as both ankles were injured I found it extremely difficult to use them.

The view from the ward was eye catching, the windows on the third floor overlooked a small lake in which fish could be seen swimming around, with a valley beyond stretching for approximately two miles, the whole scene flanked by woodland stretching up from the valley floor in a gentle slope.

On May Day I remember the inhabitants of the village came to the small lake dressed in traditional clothes to picnic and dance around ; there wasn't a uniform to be seen and one could hardly believe that this was wartime in Nazi Germany.

Several days after I arrived at Obermassfeld the time came for those who were to be repatriated to be on their way to a neutral country ; in this case Sweden, and we who would finish up in POW Camps, seeing them leave and realising they would soon be in England brought a feeling of envy.

There were some seriously ill cases in the party and we wished them a complete recovery. However it did not work out that way for some of them, because we received information several weeks later that the Peer had sadly passed away.

It was at Obermassfeld that I met three other Lancaster Pilots ; One a Wing Commander of a Pathfinder Squadron who had been shot down over Berlin the previous August, another who I had trained with in Canada, and the third an R.A.A.F. Flight Lieutenant who had also flown with a Pathfinder Squadron and had been shot down in January during the Battle of Berlin. His name was Ron King ; and he was a thoroughly nice bloke. We enjoyed each others company having the same interests in life and spent many hours talking the time away.

All four of us were blown out of our Lancasters in the same way, trying to control a blazing aircraft when the petrol tanks exploded, ejecting us through the cockpit perspex away from the disintegrating aircraft as it plunged to the ground. We assumed that is what actually happened because we were all rendered unconscious by the explosion, probably by hitting the cockpit perspex frame.

The other three all had wasted muscles in their right arm which made the arms look like drumsticks and although my arm was not affected like theirs it is a lot shorter than the other. It was a mystery how the injuries occurred.

The Wing Commander told me that Bomber Command's route to Nuremberg on the 30th March passed over Obermassfeld and he had observed the carnage of the night's operation when ninety seven Bombers were lost. He had flown more than fifty operations with the Pathfinder Force and said he had never seen so many aircraft shot down in such a short time. I told him the route over Obermassfeld was part of the 'long leg' which took us over two night fighter radio beacons and where most of the ninety seven had been destroyed.

The Wing Commander had lost his right hand when shot down and he had a hook where his hand should have been.

Ron King married a W.A.A.F. They were stationed at the same base and after the War he returned to Australia with her. Fifteen years after the War I had a surprise visit from Bill, an ex POW at Stalag Luft III, who was also an Australian and quite a character. He told me he visited Ron at his home City of Perth some years previously and they had gone out for a drink by the Harbour. As they were talking about old times Ron suddenly produced a hand gun, fired all the bullets into the sea and replaced the gun into his pocket without saying a word. Although this incident took Bill by surprise he knew that Ron's wartime experience had finally caught up with him and made him unstable. He made light of the matter and said to Ron "That was a bloody silly thing to do!" but told me he could have cried when Ron looked at him and said "Things would turn out for the best".

Soon after that Bill was told that Ron had committed suicide using the same gun. Evidently he had turned violent to his wife realised he was a danger to her and killed himself.

I only knew him as a fellow POW in Germany but as he flew forty seven operations in Bomber Command, I can vouch for the stress he must have experienced at that time and like many others must have realised what it had done to him but he killed himself.

When Ron was shot down over Berlin in January he landed in the City and was lucky to survive a hostile reception because the raid was still in progress. He was taken prisoner by the Army who took him to a hospital when the raid ended. It was a Maternity Home and he stayed

Theatre which was a P.O.W. Hospital at Meningen

there for several days during which time Bomber Command continued the raids. He was very lucky because that part of Berlin where the Maternity Home was situated escaped the concentrated carpet bombing. The City is very large and has many lakes, consequently some areas suffered more destruction than others.

During a raid, the maternity home patients were taken to the basement and Ron was left in an upper room to await whatever fate had in store for him.

I had flown on an operation to Stettin in January where the 'Graf Zeppelin', the only aircraft carrier ever built for the German Navy, was berthed waiting completion. It was our special target for the night and I remember after the raid, the Air Ministry released a target photograph to the press showing an illuminated picture of Stettin taken by a Lancaster Pathfinder crew on the night. The 'Graf Zeppelin' was smack in the middle of the photograph which had been taken by Ron's crew. Needless to say the aircraft carrier was severely damaged and took no part in the War.

Group Captain Massie, Senior British Officer at Sagan, Stalag Luft III North Compound, arrived at Obermassfeld to join the repatriation party and to our horror informed us of the murder of fifty R.A.F. Officers who had taken part in a mass escape from the Camp on the 24th March. He said he would be meeting the Foreign Minister on his arrival in England and would give him full details of the murders and the victims.

The German Commandant at Sagan had told him they were all shot whilst trying to escape when recaptured, but the Group Captain said the Commandant was very distressed on giving him the news and he was not convinced it was the truth. In Group Captain Massies' opinion there was no doubt they had been murdered and he would demand that the murderers be hunted after the War and made to pay for the murder of servicemen who were POW's within the terms of the Geneva Convention.

To return to the escape, when I arrived at Stalag Luft III some weeks later I was informed that over two hundred men were due to escape through the tunnel on the night of 24th March. I was on a raid to Berlin that night which turned out to be a costly operation for Bomber Command (I have described this raid in detail elsewhere), and as Sagan was in the warning system area for Berlin, which had a partial blackout until aircraft on a deep penetration raid approached, (Berlin had been the limit of our raids up to that time), when all lights in the area were extinguished.

The Berlin raid commenced when seventy nine prisoners out of the two hundred who were due to escape had left the tunnel, but the last man was seen by a guard who shot and injured him, then raised the alarm.

The rate of the escape through the tunnel had slowed due to the lights (powered from the mains) being extinguished and being replaced by 'home made lamps', which were made from margarine and other fats.

It was calculated that if the lights had not been extinguished many more would have escaped, but also many more would have been murdered.

I am told the fifty to be shot were selected at Gestapo Headquarters in Berlin. Identification records of the men were sent to Berlin and someone examined the pile of papers and looked at each one turning some over and saying "Kaput" or "not Kaput", at the end there were two separate piles of which those who he had described as 'Kaput' were the fifty who were eventually shot.

Whilst I was at Obermassfeld members of the Gestapo in plain clothes, came to examine the patient's lockers, it was a mystery what they were looking for but a suggestion was made that it could be for clues to the identity of Polish or Czech airmen who had flown with the R.A.F. after escaping from their respective countries when they were occupied by the Germans. When I was transferred to Stalag Luft III these searches by the Germans were commonplace, especially in one hut which housed some of these airmen who had managed to cover their identity.

During one such search at Obermassfeld a funny incident occurred when an American airman's locker was being searched by a German. The owner thought he would get away with opening his mouth and saying :

"F... Off you square headed bastard !" but the German - carrying on with his search replied without looking at the American, "I might be a square headed bastard " "but it is you that is in here, not me !" and went straight to the next locker. Nothing more was said.

I shall always remember a sergeant Air Gunner aged eighteen who was brought to the hospital after having both legs amputated above the knee when bailing out of a Halifax Bomber.

On escaping from the aircraft his legs hit a propeller which was still running and lopped off both of them.

When he wanted to move around he had to be carried and the Canadian who watched him trying to overcome his disability, sometimes by crawling on the floor, decided to do something about it and designed two home made artificial legs which he made without telling the lad.

When he brought them to the ward and told him they were for him the young lad wept tears of relief because he thought he would be legless until he returned to England. I can say there was not a dry eye in the ward when he strapped the artificial legs to the stumps of his own and took the first step with the aid of crutches. Nobody thought he would be able to succeed in walking because they were not flexible and he could only move 'stiff legged'. However he persevered and although suffering severely when the stumps of his legs were rubbed red raw, managed in time to walk with the aid of a stick.

There is a conclusion to the story and it happened like this: I regularly visit my eldest Daughter and her Husband in the village of Morcott, Rutland and sometime ago I met a chap there who was ex R.A.F. aircrew having operated on Sunderland Flying Boats in the Far East during the War. I thought as ex flyers we had talked of all our experiences but early in 1997 we were discussing various things when he mentioned a friend of his who lived in Leicester had lost both legs during the War. He said they had been cut off when he was escaping from a Bomber.

I asked him if his friend had been an Air Gunner on Halifax's and was only eighteen at the time, to which he replied that his friend had been on Halifax's and was eighteen when shot down.

I asked him if he knew whether a Canadian had made artificial legs for his friend at Obermassfeld Hospital in 1944, so then he could tell him he had been talking to someone who watched him take his first steps on them.

He said this was an amazing coincidence because his friend had been a patient at the hospital and no doubt was the same lad who I had referred to.

As the Air War over Germany in 1944 increased so did the injured aircrew coming to Obermassfeld rise, and the Germans decided to transfer many of them to a nearby Town called Meiningen, and hold them in a converted concert theatre until they were fit to be moved to a POW Camp.

I was moved there at the end of May and together with twelve American airmen ; one American Infantry Officer, One Canadian Pilot and two R.A.F. Pilots (myself and another with whom I had trained with in Canada), were put into what had been a rehearsal room overlooking a small park. The rest of the injured were put in the Auditorium.

I had the plastercast removed from my ankle at Meiningen but found it very stiff and painful when I tried to walk. This was to prove a handicap the following winter when prisoners were evacuated from Stalag Luft III in Silesia and marched for a week ; but more of that later.

I became friendly with a Sergeant from Mirfield, where my father was born, he was on the POW Medical Staff ; and they had their quarters in one of the changing rooms backstage to which I was invited. To my surprise they produced their own brew of spirits and some schnapps ; and evidently had contact with the Germans to bring them useful items to the Theatre. I think with it being a hospital, the Germans called it convalescent, security was a bit lax but everyone behaved knowing if a prisoner attempted to upset the situation, the wounded would suffer because the Germans would restrict or stop what allowance was given.

Having said that, when news came through on the secret radio that the Allies had landed in France and consolidated their beachheads, the

P.O.W. Hospital at Obermassfield is now an agricultural centre

Staff had a celebration in their own right and invited me to share in their hospitality, bringing out bottles of home brew and schnapps.

As the evening progressed so the singing became bolder and bolder ; there we were in the middle of Germany in a small room backstage of a theatre in a War, singing away songs which included 'We're going to hang out the washing on the Siegfried Line'. I do not know how we got away with it, but maybe the German staff knew the War was lost and, as the singing was not loud, let us carry on.

There was also the ritual every morning of prisoners standing at the large windows in the Gallery overlooking the main street, watching German Air Cadets marching to their training field singing songs ; the prisoners shouting through the closed windows that their chances of surviving against the R.A.F. and American Air Force were very small. Fortunately they could not be heard, here again such action was unbelievably allowed.

I remember there was a warning notice in one of the toilets and I still do not know who it was meant for ; if for the prisoners why was it allowed to remain ? It read :

"A wise old owl sat on an oak
the more he saw the less he spoke,
The less he spoke the more he heard
Oh airmen imitate that little bird".

On reflection I think it was a warning to prisoners, but could be applied to the German personnel to keep their ears open.

The American Infantry Officer who had been wounded in Italy had somehow been placed with American Air Force prisoners and had finished up with them at Obermassfeld. He was a very funny man and he could tell a story.

Every night after lights out there was always banter between the Americans; as mentioned previously there were only three non-Americans in the room.

On one particular night he related a story about the time Orson Wells produced a programme on radio, pre war, which was about the Martians landing in New York State. He must have made it convincing because he caused panic all over America, the reason being that millions missed the introduction to the programme which said it was fiction.

Anyhow our American friend was a Corporal in the Army at that time and he was I/C Guard Duty at the Camp. What followed was hilarious as he told the story.

Nobody at the Camp was listening to the radio so were not aware of the broadcast produced by Orson Wells.

The American had a girlfriend who lived on the other side of the Hudson River and as the Guard at the Camp was never called out he decided to visit her and be back well before his duty finished.

On the way to the ferry by foot he met hundreds of people running the opposite way and with them bits of conversation which made him think they were all mad ; about seeing lights in the sky.

When he arrived at the river many boats were carrying people from the other side and when one landed he asked the occupants what all the panic was about.

The answer he got was " The Martians have landed upstate, they are advancing towards New York, nobody can stop them, the Army is useless".

For a moment he thought about his absence as Guard Commander when the Martians had landed and he would not be able to call out the Guard to alert the defences. In those days he did not think there were enough rifles at the Camp for everyone.

He then found himself looking at the sky for mysterious flashes and still there was panic all round him as people fled from the direction of the 'invasion'. Some saying they ought to go back and wait for the little men (Martians) coming as they may be friendly and intend no harm. Everyone thought they were little men of peculiar appearance.

The American then decided to return to Camp and turn out the Guard because he thought when the Martians arrived at the main gate and saw how America was prepared they would laugh themselves to death. This chap had quite a sense of humour and was beginning to think that everything was too far fetched for it to be real and whoever the hoaxer was had certainly panicked thousands of people.

He returned to Camp and on his way the crowds disappeared so by the time he arrived everything was quiet. He went to the Guard House and asked why no one was preparing for the Martian invasion ; he was then told with some hilarity about the broadcast and the affect it had made, not only on New York but on the whole Country, with many of the people having heart attacks through fright.

It made Orson Wells famous but there was some talk of him being prosecuted, a step which was not taken because there had been a warning before the programme.

The conditions at Meiningen were comfortable and discipline as I have described was not severe, in fact a holiday Camp atmosphere compared with security at Stalag Luft III where I was to be transferred in July 1944.

Chapter 10

Stalag Luft III Sagan

The train journey from Meiningen to Sagan where Stalag Luft III Prisoner of War Camp for Allied Officers was situated took twenty four hours, with stops at Leipzig and Berlin.

When I was told our group of prisoners would be travelling through those two Cities, which had both suffered heavy damages and casualties from Allied bombing, I asked the RAMC Sergeant if he would exchange battle dress tops so I would be wearing khaki and he could keep my R.A.F. tunic with pilots brevy. He knew there was some feeling against allied airmen in some towns and cities and had no hesitation in letting me have his khaki top.

We departed from Meiningen on a Saturday morning and arrived at Leipzig in the middle of the afternoon, after a slow journey which was a result of bomb damage to the railway. One of the Guards, who was in his forties, met his wife and young daughter at the station and the other guard took us into a Canteen for hot drinks.

The lady behind the counter was quite pleasant and tried to communicate with us, but suddenly she started shouting and screaming and waving her arms at us and would have thrown things if we had not been removed by our escort.

What happened was that when we went into the Canteen the lady thought we were French workers who had been sent to Germany to work on munitions, but then someone mentioned we were British and American airmen POW's whereupon she went berserk. When you saw the damage around the station you couldn't blame her, but the station had hardly been damaged.

After leaving Leipzig our journey was still delayed because of bomb damage but we eventually arrived in Berlin at about 9.30pm, still in daylight.

Again we were taken to a Canteen on the station to eat the food we had prepared at Meiningen ; black bread sandwiches and coffee from Red Cross parcels. We were all feeling tired and put our heads on the table so we could have a sleep.

There were some Ukrainians in the Canteen ; these people were volunteers brought to Germany with their families to work on munitions and other work when their Country was overrun, and were passing through Berlin on their way to another town. They had OST printed on a round patch of material on their backs to identify them and this group also had small children with them.

They all looked as though they were not receiving sufficient food and as they were near us, we whispered to each other that they would probably be thankful for some of ours, even if we could not give them much.

86

Identification card Stalag Luft III

We started to pass the food under the tables, they soon realised what we were doing and held out their hands, thankful for the food.

We tried to conceal passing it, but one blonde young German soldier, a Corporal about twenty years of age, saw us and the look in his eyes was of someone who had just broken a spy ring. He was a 'hero' and started shouting hysterically about what he had seen, at the same time drawing his revolver. Things again looked very nasty and the Ukrainians were frightened to death, as he was really hysterical. We expected him blasting away but fortunately one of our guards must have told him to calm down because he put the gun back in the holster but continued shouting.

He must have used his rank on our escort because we were quickly moved to a cleaners hut, locked in with some rodents, probably rats, to keep us company until the morning, when we continued our journey to Sagan.

Stalag Luft III situated eighty miles south east of Berlin was built as a result of an agreement between Herman Goring, Marshall of the Luftwaffe, and the R.A.F. that each Service would hold and be responsible, under the Geneva Convention, for all enemy aircrew shot down and taken prisoner.

Our party of five arrived one late Sunday morning in July, and it was always the practice of prisoners at the Camp to congregate at the gates to welcome the newcomers and maybe recognise some fellow officers from their Squadrons.

Stalag Luft III contained five compounds ; Central, North, South, East and West. In 1944 the Americans were the full occupants of the South and West compound, and the North compound, where I was held, had R.A.F., Dominion and Colonial Air Force Officers, but as the Americans were being shot down in increasing numbers in late 1943/44 a large number of them were brought to the North compound.

I think there were about twelve huts all sectioned off into rooms off a long corridor, which housed four Officers when the compound opened, but in 1944 this number had increased to eight. there were three R.A.F., two R.A.A.F. and one R.C.A.F. Officers, and two American Air Force Officers in our room in hut 107, each sleeping in three tier bunks.

One of the R.A.F. Officers was a member of the Security Committee chaired by Big X ; all plans for any escapes had to be vetted by them, but after the Great Escape in March 1944 as a result of which fifty Officers were murdered, all escapes from the Camp were stopped.

There was also a Theatre and a cook house where German music and propaganda were continuously played over loud speakers on the outside walls.

In July 1944 each prisoner received one Red Cross parcel per week, i.e. British, Canadian or American, which was handed to the Officer in charge of a room making eight in all for the occupants, one of whom volunteered for cooking, this duty was accomplished in a separate kitchen in the hut.

Each week everyone looked forward to the distribution of parcels which was preceded by a voice shouting down the corridor in the hut "Parcels up !".

There was also a washroom for personal hygiene including a home made shower which was accomplished by fastening a tin, pierced with holes, onto a tap and then used as a cold shower by turning the tap fully on.

In addition all prisoners had one hot shower a week.

Laundry was also carried out in the washroom.

I was the cook in our room and kitchen facilities were available at an allotted time to each room. It was surprising what dishes could be made with food from eight parcels plus potatoes, and very infrequently a portion of raw mincemeat supplied by the Germans. We were also supplied with ersatz jam and something called fish/cheese (which had a horrible smell but nevertheless eaten).

The drama society produced some very good plays and revues, with all music, words and scripts written by members. Several of the players made a name for themselves after the War, i.e. Rupert Davies (Maigret), Peter Butterworth (Carry On films), Kenneth Mackintosh (National Theatre - Shakesperian Actor), John Casson (Son of Dame Sybil Thorndike and Lewis Casson) also produced Joan of Arc (A play made famous by his Mother) in the Camp Theatre.

I remember the production of Joan of Arc, John Casson who I believe was a Lieutenant Commander in the Fleet Air Arm had the play sent to him from England, and he cast a New Zealand Pilot in the main role. The two of them would often walk round the 'circuit' rehearsing his part.

The circuit was the name of a complete walk around the perimeter of the compound just inside the trip wire which was a border of wood sections, six inches wide, fastened horizontally about a foot from the ground.

They walked round the circuit for several weeks before the play opened and the pilot who was on stage for a total of approximately three hours at various times was very good.

The three actors mentioned previously also took principal parts.

Many years after the War I saw Peter Butterworth and his wife Janet Brown in Scarborough, where he was appearing in one of the 'Carry on' plays during the summer season. We reminisced about the days in Stalag Luft III where he was a prisoner a lot longer than I, having been shot down early in the War when he was a pilot in the Fleet Air Arm.

Rupert Davies was also in the Fleet Air Arm.

Peter died not long afterwards, but I saw Janet Brown some years after in Port o Pollensa, Majorca. We were discussing his roles during captivity and I told her he played Robertson Hares' characters in the Ben Travers farces at the Camp Theatre ; she took some convincing because Peter had a full head of hair but did the characters wonderfully under his bald headed wig.

On my first day in the Compound after I was introduced to my room mates and settled in, I wandered on to the playing field where a cricket match was in progress between England and Australia (there was a large number of R.A.A.F. Officers in the Camp) and the field was part of the compound about 120^2 yds.

England were batting and on looking to the middle I saw a familiar figure at the crease. It was Nigel Bloy one of my room mates who was a navigator at Metheringham, where we discussed the chances of survival if shot down. When I saw him safe and well I wondered what had happened to Chubb, his Bomb Aimer who said he would jump out of the aircraft straight away if given the chance.

As I was pondering the question a voice next to me said, in a surprised way, "I can't believe it !" and on turning to the speaker saw it was Chubb. We were both as surprised but thankful that all three of us had survived and naturally I asked him the obvious question, "At what height did you bail out ?".

Without hesitation he replied "About fifteen thousand feet and I got away with it".

He told me his Pilot Dicky Legget, who I knew very well on the Squadron, was killed.

After the War Nigel Bloy played County cricket for Hampshire.

We had two roll-calls a day in the North Compound, they were called Appels, one first thing in the morning and the other in daylight at about 5pm. Prisoners were grouped according to hut numbers around the sports field which was an area of sandy soil on one side of the Compound.

A roll-call, or appel, could be a very slow job because the Germans very often decided to search the rooms and we could be left standing for several hours.

When we returned to the hut all the bedding and other loose items were piled in a heap on the floor.

The Germans were very strong on security, because it was from the North Compound that the Great Escape was made. They also had a crack body of Wermach troops at the ready, with orders to shoot if any major incident occurred or if a single escapee was captured. It was a very dangerous time and we all had to be careful.

I remember when the Americans extended their daylight raids and flew over Silesia, prisoners had to return to their huts if the siren sounded and on one occasion an American in the South Compound who was looking out of an unopened window from well inside the room, was shot dead by one of the guards in a sentry tower.

There were also 'Ferrets' employed in the Compounds to keep an eye open for any suspicious sign that the 'Kriegies' as we were known amongst ourselves, were not up to any mischief. These men were Luftwaffe personnel who walked around in overalls and forage caps. Some of them were very competent and we had to be very careful when they were in the Compound or walking through the corridors in the block.

I remember one of the ferrets was called 'Adolf' by the prisoners, he had a reputation for his dedication to duty and he would go into all corners of the Camp to try and find anything he might think required further investigation by his superiors.

Adolf was a ferret who had no sense of humour and because of his hero worship of the Fuhrer and his Hitler look-alike moustache, was the target of many a trick played by the kriegies, of which there were many.

Some of the other ferrets had a sense of humour and some could be bribed with chocolate and cigarettes from Red Cross parcels, but this was only done by their contact prisoners who could speak German, and were nominated by the Escape Committee to make the liaison. No one else was allowed to speak to the ferrets.

With the approach of winter in Silesia temperatures dropped as the winds came from the east across Poland over the flat landscape.

The snow fell and stayed on the ground. We had no fuel for the stoves in the rooms in the winter of 1944/45 and you put extra clothes on to go to bed more than you wore during the day, when people walked round the circuit to keep warm. There was always one continuous body of men going round and round the circuit ; as one stepped out another would take his place and prisoners wore all types of clothing to keep warm.

To go back to the trip wire around the Compound and what it was there for. It was certainly part of security and very dangerous territory if rules were not followed.

For instance when a cricket match was played , or any other ball game, it was not always possible to prevent the ball going over the trip wire and stopping in the area between it and the barbed wire.

There were three sentry boxes (Goon boxes as we called them) situated on each side of the Compound, one at either corner and one in the middle of the fence.

If a player wished to retrieve a ball he had to wait on the outside of the trip wire, attract the attention of each guard in all three sentry boxes which could be seen on that side and wait for them to give him permission to cross the trip wire and retrieve the ball. To do this he donned a white coat, not unlike a cricket umpires, with a red spot about four inches diameter on the back. These guards were all trigger happy operators of automatic weapons and it was fatal not to follow the procedure.

A secret radio was operated every day to receive news from the BBC ; which was dismantled after use.

The news was read in the corridor of each hut in the evenings, with look outs posted to make sure no ferrets entered. They were always walking through but as soon as they put one foot in the block a voice from somewhere would shout 'Goon in the Block'.

I think the Germans thought we were operating a concealed switch by foot because as soon as they entered a warning voice rang out.

About eight weeks after my arrival I was called to the Forelager ; this was an enclosure between the main gate and the Compound where the German administration and sick quarters were situated.

My Dad had evidently been notified of my survival, although injured, and he had asked the Red Cross to let him know the extent of my injuries.

At least I knew that whatever happened in the future my family would know I was currently alive. The injuries to my ankles had made them stiff and sore and I realised I would not be able to play any more ball games ; my neck was also stiff and I still could not raise my head at all above eye level.

The escapees who were lucky enough to survive the Great Escape Massacre returned to the Compound and one of them told me that when recaptured they were held in cells at a Gestapo Centre in Glogau. Some were systematically separated and moved from the cells, being told they were going back to Sagan, but finished up shot in the back after being taken for 'a ride'.

The others were beginning to worry because they were in the hands of the Gestapo, who ignored the Geneva Convention, and did not give any information to the Red Cross about prisoners.

I have already described how the prisoners for execution were selected. The news of the murder of the fifty Officers was not only received with horror by the prisoners, but the German Commandant who gave the news to the Senior British Officer ; Group Captain Massie, was also shaken ; it was the Commandants' last duty before being transferred, probably to the Russian front.

Later in 1944 the ashes of the fifty Officers were returned to the Camp and handed over to the Senior British Officer who was allowed to place the urns in a shelter made by the prisoners in Sagan cemetery.

A Roll of Honour was placed in the cemetery after the War.

A ban was put on all further escapes until things quietened down but after the massacre no one had any intention of trying to get away.

There was one attempted escape however by a prisoner, he was known to be a little unstable and at the time was watching some Russian prisoners clearing empty Red Cross tins from a small enclosure in the Compound.

The Russians moved the cans on a horse drawn cart to a site outside the Camp, and as this chap was watching he suddenly jumped on the cart whilst the German driver's attention was elsewhere. At that point he was lucky that the Russians co-operated and in no time had him covered with tin cans.

The German driver had not seen the incident and when the cart was full drove it away carrying the two Russians and the kriegie through the gates where it was soon clear of the Camp.

Everyone wondered if by some miracle he might get away and for a couple of hours fingers were kept crossed, not only for him to make it, but if recaptured that no harm would befall him.

Anyhow hope turned to disappointment when he returned to the Camp escorted by two guards and taken straight to the cooler. Evidently what had happened must have been very funny because when the cart arrived at the tip, and the driver manoeuvred it to upturn the contents on to a large tip, the fellow came off with a load and finished upside down with his legs sticking out of a stack of tins.

Through the summer and autumn as the Camp received news by BBC of the Russian advance it was becoming increasingly apparent that they would be approaching the Camp before many more weeks. If that happened the prisoners would be at the mercy of the German Army and so it was planned for a tunnel to be driven to the Armoury so that the Camp could be protected if it became necessary, we knew however that our chances of survival would be very limited.

Major Low of the United States 8th Air Force, lived in the room next to ours. He flew Liberators and was a Flight Commander on the Squadron led by Colonel Jimmy Stewart, the film star who completed twenty missions over Germany during the heavy battles of late 1943/44. I was an admirer of the Colonel both as a film star and a combat flyer, and as Major Low and he used to socialise in their off duty hours he told me of some of their times together.

Evidently Jimmy Stewart wrote only to two ladies whilst in England, one was his Mother and the other Olivia de Havilland.

He was only once recognised by the young ladies of Norwich (where he was stationed), in a cinema when the lights came on at the interval. It was his practice to sit very low in his seat and put his cap over his eyes pretending to be asleep during an interval, but on this occasion he was recognised and together with his companions was chased outside into the blackout where they located their jeep and drove away.

He made many films after the War but had a clause in his contract with the studio that no reference was to be made about his War Service. The film I shall always remember was 'It's a Wonderful Life' which he made about forty years ago.

When the number of Americans in the Camp increased they started to participate in the recreational activities of the Compound and it was not long before they were ready to produce a play in the Camp Theatre. The play chosen was 'Front Page' which was well known in the States having been produced on Broadway.

One of the American occupants of our room was called Robert Taylor, the same name as a famous Hollywood Heart Throb in the 1930's and 40's.

He told me that when stationed in England, and visited the nearest town, his crew would ask the girls if they would like to meet Robert Taylor.

Of course they expected to see the Film Star but when he appeared he was greeted with 'who are you kidding' by them. He was however a good looking lad who had some acting experience, having lived in Hollywood and his Father was a lecturer at the Southern Californian University.

His part in the production of 'Front Page' was that of a prostitute, and like the main character in Joan of Arc we walked round the Compound as I assisted him with his lines.

The production never reached the stage because we evacuated the Camp as the Russians advanced.

I never saw Robert Taylor again but soon after I was repatriated received an invitation to his wedding which I was not able to accept because of travelling restrictions in the aftermath of the War.

Whilst I reminisce about the U.S.A.A.F. prisoners of War in Germany I also remember a meeting with an ex Luftwaffe pilot whilst on holiday in Austria in the 1960's.

My Wife and I were in a party touring the Austrian Tyrol and on one particular journey our bus stopped at a restaurant which was situated on a mountain at an altitude of 8,000ft.

After ordering refreshments we sat at a table occupied by a very tall man, who from time to time rubbed his forehead and said in broken

English that "The lack of oxygen was giving him a headache". I sympathised with him and asked what brought him to such a high altitude. He said he was a Hydro-Electrical Engineer whose work took him to such high places.

I then asked him where he had learned to speak English and to my surprise he answered "Me no like Bostons". It came to me that he must have been shot down by a Boston aircraft of the U.S.A.A.F., taken as a P.O.W. and sent to the U.S.A. where thousands of Germans were held captive in Texas. He confirmed my assumption and said he served in the Luftwaffe flying Me. 109's in North Africa, was shot down by a Boston, taken prisoner and sent to the U.S.A.

I told him I did not like Me. 110's having been shot down in a Lancaster by one and taken to prison camps in Germany. After sympathising with each other we exchanged experiences in the Air War and spoke for some minutes before he bade farewell and went on his way.

I never thought I would meet an Austrian ex Luftwaffe pilot on a remote mountain in Austria, who had been shot down by the Allies.

All the huts in the North Compound were raised about eighteen inches from the ground which made it very difficult to drive a tunnel, the ones driven for the Great Escape went down the inside of the footings of a stove before travelling horizontally.

However the incident I am about to describe does not relate to any escape.

It occurred after heavy snow had fallen and was packed all around the huts where it froze and became solid. There were two access points from underneath the hut, one each at opposite corners, and on one occasion a ferret was noticed to enter one access where he would crawl through slowly listening to prisoners talking in their rooms and then exit on hands and knees at the opposite end.

When he had been under the hut for about a minute both access points were closed by packing them with ice and snow so when the ferret came to emerge he could not do so and without tools could not get out. The temperature was below freezing and he soon became very cold and started shouting and thumping the floor to attract attention. The prisoners raised their voices, some singing and left the ferret to his icy cell for some time until they thought he would be really cold and released him.

We didn't see a ferret crawl under a hut again because shortly after we were evacuated.

One story that was related to Stalag Luft III during an appel was about the German Officer taking a roll-call. After he had finished counting he read out the 'riot act' which contained restrictions on prisoners' activities, e.g. library closure. Every time he announced a penalty the prisoners cheered ; and he became so exasperated at this reception that he shouted at them in English :

"You English are all the same, you think we Germans know

f... nothing, but we know f... all"
at which there was an uproar from hundreds of prisoners.

In September 1944 it was obvious our Red Cross parcels were not arriving in the Camp regularly due to rail transport in Germany being disrupted by Allied bombing. These parcels came from either Sweden or Switzerland and it was possible that the Germans would stop them altogether if they realised the War was lost and the population could not be properly fed as the Country was decimated. They might even confiscate Red Cross parcels at the Camp and distribute them to the local people.

A decision was made by the Germans to cut the prisoners rations from one Red Cross parcel per man to one parcel between two men, one parcel for one man was hardly enough to maintain sufficient nutrition but half of one would not be enough to feed a man through the winter.

Christmas 1944 came and brought optimism to the Camp because according to the news on the BBC the Russians were advancing ever nearer to the River Oder (fifty miles from the Camp), their last big obstacle before the drive to Berlin.

The last few months had seen them enter Poland and East Prussia and everyone wondered if they would cross the River Oder and release the Camp, or would the Germans evacuate Stalag Luft III where ten thousand prisoners were held.

The latter action would cause chaos on the roads because the snow had arrived and storms were regularly sweeping across the Silesian Plain dropping temperatures to - 20°. It could be that the Germans might take drastic action against us now the War was lost ; in fact after the War I read an article in which Goebels had suggested that Germany withdraw from the Geneva Convention, but when the Allied Governments heard about this threat, they warned the Germans such action would have very serious consequences.

Some prisoners thought that as the Russians were advancing rapidly there might not be time for the Camp to be evacuated, and prisoners could be armed by breaking into the Armoury from the tunnel which was ready to make the breakthrough.

When diggers worked in the tunnel, other prisoners were detailed to keep watch on the ferrets as they entered and left the compound ; if they came anywhere near the building from which the tunnel was being driven, signals would be given by the look-outs and operations stopped for the time being.

Timber to shore the tunnel was taken from prisoners bunks, and I remember I was down to five boards and felt very insecure when lying in mine. One night the inevitable happened I fell through from my top bunk, crashed on to the person below, and then on to the man in the bottom bunk. I think this was a scene often repeated in other rooms.

It was now mid January and the Russians were fast approaching the River Oder but there was no sound of artillery fire or signs of fires glowing in the night sky. The Germans starting flying offensive operations from an aerodrome near Sagan with all types of aircraft. They took off with bombs to fly east ; within a short time explosions were heard as they bombed to break the ice to stop the Russian tanks crossing the river. They were back within thirty minutes so from the time it took them to fly back we had an idea how far away the Russians were.

We realised the time was approaching when the Germans would have to make a decision about us and everyone was praying they would abandon the Camp, even if it meant we would be in the thick of the fighting.

Plans were made to show it was a Prisoner of War Camp by placing huge letters 'POW' which could be seen from the air.

Chapter 11

Survival march from Stalag Luft III, January 1945

I remember a Saturday in the latter part of January 1945 ; the weather was bitterly cold with temperatures well below zero and aircraft continued bombing the ice packed River Oder.

When night came we knew something was about to happen and about 10pm the order came that all prisoners at Stalag Luft III would commence evacuating the Camp at 12 midnight with three Red cross parcels to two prisoners.

A frenzy of activity commenced as prisoners made sledges to carry their belongings on the march westward, away from the Russians. Everyone had mementoes which they would take with them, but the most important item was enough clothing in which to keep warm because we had no idea of our destination or how long we would be marching.

When the time came to leave the Camp I knew of two people who decided to hide there with sufficient rations, and hope the Russians would soon reach Sagan and free them. I don't know what happened to them because 'Uncle Joe' as we called Joe Stalin ordered his armies to stop at the River Oder.

The North Compound column commenced moving about twelve midnight and what a collection of clothing the men were wearing, I had seen pictures of Germans taken prisoner at Stalingrad in winter 1943, wearing anything that would keep out the cold and we were just the same.

The weather was atrocious as we slowly moved west, and nobody thought the Germans had any idea of what to do with us. The temperature was -20° with the snow driving horizontally across the Silesian Plain, and even the German guards, who were not young men, were unhappy and miserable.

We travelled for about sixteen hours with several stops and now and again some members of our column would see an old Squadron colleague in another column, with remarks like "It's a long walk to Lincoln".

At 4 o'clock in the afternoon the column stopped at a desolate village with farm buildings on either side of the road. By this time the prisoners were freezing in the bitterly cold wind and were wondering when they would be found shelter. Word was eventually passed down the line that men in front were being moved into farm buildings, but as I was near the back, I had to wait a long time with the remainder before it was our turn. By that time all the farm buildings were full of men and farm animals and it looked as though we would not be given shelter. I do not think the Germans could have cared less whether we survived or not, and even the guards were muttering that it was not the way to treat human beings. I think that is why they put us in with the animals.

The guards were not supplied with adequate clothing to keep them warm because the best protective gear was sent to the Russian Front for the fighting troops.

We were eventually put into a large building which sheltered animals from the cold Silesian winter. Scores of men from the front of the column were already housed there and had spread out as much as they could to bed down for the night.

When we arrived they had been in the building for nearly an hour and we had to find room the best way we could. The building was separated into pens for farm animals, i.e. pigs, sheep, cattle, horses, the lot and the prisoners had spread themselves out, even sleeping in the pens on clean straw. I bedded down with several others in a strip between two pens, with sheep that were restless. Not only that but three or four horses were tethered about 3yds from where we slept and they were continuously pawing with their hooves and moving around.

It was not an ideal place for exhausted men who had marched twelve hours in atrocious conditions. However the night passed without any accidents and we rose and left our 'bed mates' at 4 o' clock the next morning.

Our ablutions were carried out with ice cold water and hot water was provided for us to make drinks from tea and coffee from the Red Cross parcels which we were pulling on home made sledges.

The march continued in the same way for two more days by which time we knew the Russians had not advanced beyond the River Oder, where they would stay until the spring offensive.

Spirits were very low but on the fourth day we arrived at a French Labour Camp to rest overnight and slept on the floor. There was also a doctor who treated some of the effects of the march on men's feet ; several had suffered frost bite.

The injuries to my neck, back, ankles and knees which I suffered when shot down were aggravated and I had marched without being able to lift my head above eye level. My ankles were swollen and I did not take off my boots during the march, otherwise I would not have been able to get them back on again ; that would have meant being left by the wayside with doubts about my survival because there had been gun fire along the route, and rumour had it that those not able to carry on were shot.

It was on this part of the march that I was amazed to see two prisoners riding what appeared to be a 'shire' type of horse, which the farmers had let them have at our first stop, evidently because of his uncertain future and efficient bartering by the men with some contents of their food parcels.

The French doctor at the labour Camp advised me to leave my footwear alone for a few days before washing my feet, he suggested my ankles would probably lose the swelling by that time.

On the fourth day we stopped at a small town and were put into a building, like a palatial stable for thoroughbred horses, on a large estate. We were supplied with fresh straw and for the first time in four days were allowed to sleep off the effects of twelve hour marches in a heated building.

Whilst I was there I did my first bartering with a house frau who lived in one of the cottages on the estate, I gave her a packet of dried prunes and she gave me a loaf of black bread in return.

The surprising part of our stay there was the area of movement we were allowed, we could not go into the main street but many people came on to the estate, and I do not think they would accept the situation of the Russians arriving at the River Oder. It could have been they believed all they heard on the German radio which turned defeat into victory.

I remember the noise of what seemed to be motorcycle engines coming from the area, and was told by a German, with a glint in his eyes, that they would soon carry a bomb and crash onto London. He meant the V1 and a factory making the engines was next door to the estate, the noise we heard was of them being tested.

It was in this town called Muskau where we encountered troops from the Herman Goring Division who were moving up to meet the Russians. They were fine looking young men, similar to the British Guards and although they said Germany would win the War you could sense they thought otherwise.

They acknowledged that when we were shot down the War for us was over and our survival would be assured, but if they were ordered to shoot all prisoners they would do so without hesitation. It was very frightening but I wonder how many of them survived.

We had been marching for five days in ice and snow and low temperatures when the weather suddenly took an unexpected change and the temperature rose to above freezing point for the first time. The sledges were no longer required and we carried what food was left from the Red Cross parcels on our backs.

The next point of our march was a railway marshalling yard, not very big because it had not been visited by the Russian Air Force ; not a plane had been seen during the march, possibly because of the bad weather.

Thousands of German troops were waiting at the railway yard for transport to the Russian Front. There were many young boys amongst them who were on the point of dying for the Fuhrer. They were fanatical and would go to their death with all the false teachings of the Hitler youth.

Once the Russians started their Spring Offensive ; there would be no stopping them and as the British and American Armies advanced from the West, German territory would gradually narrow with us somewhere in the middle. When this happened all we could hope for was that at the

Everyone knew the most dangerous part of our captivity was about to start ; when the time came would the Germans act within the rules of the Geneva Convention or would orders be given for us to be executed ? After all the killing of helpless people, especially in Russia, had not been a problem for them.

After nearly a week on the road on what had been a fight for survival due to the weather conditions, frostbite and existing injuries trying to keep with the column, the march ended. We never did confirm that people were shot because they could not overcome the conditions and fell out ; but rifle fire was heard at points on the route.

Chapter 12

Luckenwald

Several hundred of us were put into cattle trucks at the marshalling yard to be taken to Luckenwald, a Prisoner of War Camp and Labour Camp combined. It was situated about forty miles south of Berlin and held twenty eight thousand POW's and labour workers from occupied countries, plus Russian POW's who were not protected by the Geneva Convention because their Country was not a signatory to it. The Town of Luckenwald was one mile south of the Camp.

Although the journey was not very far it took twelve hours to cover the distance ; the railways were now being bombed at such a rate that in a short time they would be unworkable.

The Camp was like a small town with barbed wire fences round the compounds and outer perimeter. Numerous sentry boxes were also positioned around the perimeter and the usual guard dogs with their handlers patrolled day and night.

Prisoners were housed in barracks with earth floors and slept in wooden bunks eight tiers high in blocks of twenty four ; there was hardly room to move.

It was soon obvious that all POW's from Stalag Luft III had not come to Luckenwald ; and a week or so after we arrived word came from the Germans that most of them had been sent to a Camp in North Germany.

They would eventually be freed by the British Second Army and transferred home immediately ; whereas we at Luckenwald were in for some dangerous and frustrating times before freedom came.

The residue of the Red Cross parcels carried on the march were soon gone and we were to live on a slice of black bread about an inch thick, five potatoes (most of them black) and a pint of warm water ; daily. Cold water was always available on tap, but there was to be no further supplies of Red Cross parcels.

The weather was cold, but thankfully there was very little snow, and people would stay in bed to keep warm. There was nothing to get up for and moral was low ; the only thing to look forward to was the Russian Spring Offensive even though we knew we would be in the thick of the fighting. What exercise people could manage was walking ; and after life in an aircrew prison Camp it was strange to be amongst civilian workers who were deported from their own countries and sent to Luckenwald.

A lot of them managed to obtain supplies of food and would come into our barracks at night to barter ; they thought they were on to a good thing by offering someone a small amount of food for a watch ; but this type of bartering was soon stopped when they were shown 'the door'.

I became friendly with a Polish Fighter pilot who escaped to England from his Country when it was overrun and joined the Free Polish Air Force.

He was of aristocracy, a Count, and flew in the Battle of Britain shooting down several German aircraft before he was shot down himself.

He managed to keep out of the Gestapo's hands who were always trying to identify these men as 100% Polish ; but they had been given British Citizenship which the Germans were always trying to disprove.

I had always been interested in choral singing and some of the civilians in the compound were Polish who had formed a male voice choir which sang every night. They were quite good and I asked my Polish friend if he would ask the conductor, who was a member of the Warsaw Symphony Orchestra, to invite me to listen to them

I do not know what they said to each other because when I arrived for their practice and was introduced I expected to sit on one side and enjoy the singing.

However when the Conductor shook hands he then led me to the Group, who had smiles of welcome on their faces, and put me amongst their ranks.

I knew it would be useless for me to join in because I couldn't speak a word of Polish, but then the choir struck up with a Norwegian song ; so there I was an Englishman in a Polish Choir, which was singing in Norwegian. Nevertheless I enjoyed it because they were very good.

My friend the Polish Fighter pilot spent his leaves with a wartime member of the Cabinet.

February came and March but still no sign of the Russian Offensive, although the American Air Force flew over nearly every day and the R.A.F. bombed Potsdam at night, which was twenty miles North and everything seemed to be happening on the doorstep. I now saw and heard the effects of a Bomber Command Raid from the ground and it was very spectacular.

One morning there was a commotion in the compound and the men gathered round a large man in civilian clothes and Homburg hat. It was Max Schmelling, the heavyweight boxer who had knocked out Joe Louis for the World Heavyweight Championship before the War. This had been against all odds but Louis regained the Championship the following year when he knocked out Max Schmelling.

However for a time it gave Hitler and the Germans time to gloat over Schmelling's victory ; they told the World the German race produced champions and were particularly boastful because their boxer had beaten a black man.

I think the reason for Schmelling's visit to the Camp was that he knew Germany had lost the War and was showing sympathy for the Allied prisoners, hoping his name would find favour with the Allies to give him a position in a Post War German administration, and also making signs that he was not a Nazi. It might have done him some good because he was allowed to open a night-club in Cologne immediately after the War. The Senior British Officer at the Camp was a Group Captain and one day in March we heard he had been moved and was on his way to Bavaria. The reason for the move was that the Germans were transferring all high ranking R.A.F. and American Air Force Officers to the Bavarian mountains where they would be held as hostages.

It was known some of the Nazi Hierarchy were in no mood to allow the release of aircrew because of the damage inflicted on the Third Reich by them which had been enormous ; the air war was fought continuously over five years and the R.A.F. and American Air Force had complete mastery over Germany in the last weeks of the War.

The rest of us had not long to wait before the Germans gave notice to the acting S.B.O. that all aircrew officers were to be ready to leave the Camp almost immediately.

A roll-call was taken and about four hundred officers were marched to Luckenwald Station to board cattle trucks waiting in the sidings. We were to follow the Group Captain to Bavaria and be held hostage in the mountains. It was the worst part of my captivity up to then. I had been blown out of an exploding Lancaster with full petrol and bomb loads and survived a march in atrocious conditions from Stalag Luft III only to be held hostage at the end of the War by a fanatical and tyrannical regime who would show no mercy.

The cattle trucks were stationed in sidings and the Germans allowed us to place white sheets with POW painted on them on the top of each cattle truck, in case the Americans with their daylight activity were out strafing the railways.

We did not move from the sidings and were puzzled as to why the delay, but as long as we remained there we hoped the Germans might change their minds.

The local people were curious and came to look at us in the railway cutting where the trucks were standing. There were no toilet facilities and this duty was also watched with some amusement by the locals.

At night we were locked in the cattle trucks and waited for the train to pull out but it remained stationary.

The next morning a train from Berlin arrived at Luckenwald Station and I had never seen anything like it. Passengers were not only in the carriages but hanging on to the doors outside the train, sitting on the buffers cowboy fashion and were even on the carriage roofs.

There was also three anti aircraft positions each with four mounted guns, one behind the engine, one in the middle and one at the end of the train.

The part of Germany which was still in their hands was now only a corridor about a hundred miles wide, but at least one train was still running.

There was to be plenty of excitement though within the next few minutes because prior to the train arriving we had observed American Thunderbolt strafing planes circling the railway lines about two miles down the track.

They must have seen the Red Cross signs otherwise they would have attacked the train whilst it was standing in the station.

It was amazing because the train steamed out heading straight for the waiting planes with all the passengers sitting in their original positions.

As it left the station all eyes were turned in that direction and although it disappeared from view, soon arrived at the point where the planes were circling.

We then saw the planes diving and heard the firing of machine guns and

cannon ; at the same time tracer bullets from the gun crews could be seen arching their way towards the planes but it was not long before the attacking aircraft scored direct hits because there was an explosion and a huge volume of steam rose to the sky.

The attack lasted several minutes before the planes flew off leaving one train badly damaged or destroyed ; there must have been hundreds of casualties.

No Luftwaffe aircraft were seen during the attack and it was obvious that the American Air Force had complete mastery of the skies over what was left of the Third Reich.

At the end of two days waiting in the cattle trucks there was still no sign of our moving and we wondered if the Allied advance on the Western front had made the Germans alter their plans. This soon became the reason because General Patton, who was in command of the American Army in the Southern part of the front, had met with little resistance when he sent his spearhead forward ; so he ordered them to continue, and in so doing had cut communications to the South, thus stopping our movement to Bavaria.

It was with relief and prayers of thanks when we marched back to the Camp, hoping that freedom would come before any further plans were made by the Germans to use us in negotiations with the Allies.

After years in captivity some of the prisoners had always thought their release would be a matter of formality, they never thought their lives would be endangered by mad men hell bent on making them suffer both mentally and physically when the War was lost.

The question on everyone's lips during the next few days was :-
"When is Uncle Joe going to start his Spring Offensive ?"

It was now April and the American Air Force continued their bombing operations every day with no opposition, apart from flak, although four aircrew were brought to the Camp after their aircraft was shot down on one of the raids. Interrogating airmen was a thing of the past because there was nowhere to take them ; they were to be POW's for the shortest period anyone was held.

The Russian Army on the Oder gave us our answer in the middle of April when they opened up with all artillery on a front between the Baltic down the River Oder to the end of the line in the South, hundreds of miles.

In the section opposite Berlin there were four hundred guns to the mile. It was the first time I had heard an artillery barrage and it was unforgettable, the explosions continued for twenty four hours and you realised why the Russians advanced very quickly at the start of a battle, they just softened up and demoralised the enemy.

Everything went quiet after twenty four hours and we expected news of the offensive would be broadcast by the BBC ; which we still received, but nothing was mentioned in the broadcasts, so there we were knowing something big had started but not quite sure what it was.

However three days after the barrage stopped a lot of smoke was seen to the East from what must have been many fires.

That night it looked as though the German soldiers and guards at the Camp were evacuating, because there was much running around with a certain amount of panic. We were locked in our barracks but people who could see the main gates said none of the Germans had left and the next day everything appeared normal.

The day after we saw history being made as smoke from both the Eastern and Western Fronts was seen on both horizons, and we hoped the Americans would arrive at the Camp before the Russians. It was not known at the time that both Armies were to stop at the River Elbe, about forty miles west of Luckenwald ; this was to put prisoners in a lot of danger and create frustration.

On a Saturday around the middle of April we finally witnessed the end of our time as Prisoners of War, when all Germans evacuated the Camp at 12.30pm. Everyone was absolutely thrilled but this was tempered by our new situation which first of all put us in no man's land, and secondly the question of how long would it be before the Russians arrived ? In the meantime there was no way we were under any protection, we were on our own.

Some organisation had been planned for every prisoner to participate in the running of the Camp if the situation arose and this was put into operation immediately. The difficulty was the large number of foreign workers and Russian POW's who could not be brought into the plans, first of all because they did not wish to participate, and secondly the Russians were hell bent on revenge for the way they had been treated in captivity and would do things their way.

I had to assist the 'telephone engineers' to sort out the Camp's switchboard which was in a state of mixed wires and plugs as everything had been left in chaos. The first job was to examine the wires outside and on starting this task we had to climb a pole which could be scaled from a low roof building.

Having got on to the roof the engineers climbed the pole to fix the wires ; the weather was misty and damp and we felt very exposed being situated somewhere between the German and Russian Armies in a silent world, you could hear a pin drop, there was not even gun fire - it was as though the World was holding its breath waiting for the next move.

In our case we had not long to wait because somewhere above the mist came the scream of a plane's engine as it dived towards us. It sounded as though it was coming straight at us and we all dived off the roof as tracer bullets raked the forest which surrounded the Camp.

We realised what dangerous work we had taken on, especially if 'caught up the pole !'.

However the state of telephones and wires required little work on them to bring them back to working conditions and our part was soon completed.

There was a cross-road half a mile from the Camp and during the afternoon a detachment of German troops arrived there and set up defences to delay the Russian advance. The Officer in charge sent for the Senior British Officer and warned him of the dangerous position the Camp was in from both sides, because if any light was seen coming from the Camp during the night he would not hesitate to fire mortar shells at us.

Everyone made sure the Camp remained in darkness, but it was very eerie because nothing relating to fighting could be heard and we wondered how long we would be in this no man's land ; the Germans having left sixteen hours ago.

No one slept that night and as dawn broke our thoughts were fixed on survival; it was as though the Germans had withdrawn and the Russians bypassed us, which would of course be the ideal way to gain our freedom.

However at 6.30am on Sunday morning a big cheer went up and on looking out of the compound down the road on the other side of the wire a Russian tank was seen approaching. It was part of a spearhead with Mongolian men and women in quilted clothing, armed to the teeth.

Some men had somehow managed to get between the inner barbed wire fence and outer fence amongst rolled barbed wire along the length of it. Other men who were fed up of the sight of barbed wire made signs to the Russians to knock down the wooden posts of the fence with their tank tracks.

They got the message and put one side of their tracks to run down all the posts; but when they started and the posts were coming down, the rolled barbed wire snaked all over the place and the men between the two barbed wire fences had to jump out of the way or else be caught in an agonising way.

As the Russians were demolishing the wire fences, automatic fire was heard and tracer bullets came out of the forest near the Camp. Everybody either dropped to the ground or sought shelter in the barracks; the Russians turned their attention to the place from where the firing came and drove the tank into the forest. The firing continued for a short time before the Russians emerged from their sortie ; there was no further gunfire.

The celebrations inside the Camp now the Russians had arrived were unforgettable, but although the Allied POW's were well organised to control the situation the Russian POW's and some foreign labour went on the rampage. This was because they had no leadership and there were too many of them to be brought into our disciplinary rules.

When the Russian spearhead continued their advance North later in the day several Russian POW's went with them and it was obvious they would soon reach the outskirts of Berlin.

No resistance except the token one near the Camp had materialised ; the German contingent at the cross-roads had moved during the night and as far as we knew there were no other defences nearby. The Town of Luckenwald would be taken but not for another day.

We were impatient to go home but would have to wait until the Russians handed us over to the Americans who were approaching the River Elbe to the West.

Not another Russian was seen that day and we went to bed wondering what fate would have in store for us the next day.

It was a moonlit night and as I dropped off into an uneasy sleep I was suddenly awakened again by the noise of a diving aircraft firing tracers between the barracks just outside the window. I dropped quickly off the bunk as did all the others, all of us finishing in a heap on the floor.

During the previous weeks many POW's had arrived at the Camp after being evacuated and the barracks were so crowded the Germans had erected marquees outside the wire, on the west side, to hold several hundred Americans. Tracer fire from the diving aircraft had strafed the ground between two marquees which were four and a half feet apart, but miraculously had not penetrated the tents.

The next day a reconnaissance party was sent into Luckenwald to find out was happening ; and they returned saying the Town was quiet as the inhabitants waited with dread for the Russians to arrive.

Twenty four hours after the main Russian Army in that sector, I believe commanded by Marshall Koniev, commenced taking the area and the fighting around Luckenwald turned out to be some of the most ferocious of the War.

We were smack in the middle of it but thank God the Russians would wait until nightfall before sorting the Germans out in the forest.

Spotlights were put over each corner of the Camp at night as Russian artillery fired round after round at their targets which seemed to be hit almost immediately.

This continued for two or three nights, and previously when we thought the Germans had left the area there must have been many thousands of them waiting in the forests to fight their last battle, because the BBC news reported that in fighting around Luckenwald sixty thousand Germans were killed and one hundred and twenty thousand taken prisoner.

We prisoners were on very dangerous ground at Luckenwald ; we had thought our captivity would end peacefully when the Germans evacuated the Camp as their Army seemed non-existent ; when we were suddenly in the middle of a big battle ; anything could have happened to us ; we were so helpless.

It depended whether or not both sides isolated us from the fighting.

The Russian Army eventually moved on leaving companies of men to mop up the Germans in the Forest. The Town was in their hands and from accounts given by parties who were sent in, there had been looting and raping before they continued their advance.

The day to day running of the Camp had not changed ; we were not allowed outside the gates but were free to wander around all the compounds where we could talk with different nationalities ; it was surprising how both participants in a conversation could understand a lot of what each other said.

The Russian Church was eye catching inside, there must have been some very artistic people amongst them because the statues and the paintings were beautiful.

Some of the Russian ex P.O.W.'s were now on duty at the Camp gates, having been put there by their Army before they pushed on, but many more than we thought had gone with the Army ; there was no question of them volunteering, as far as the Russian Army were concerned, if the men were told to pick up their arms again they did so, or were shot. No doubt many of them were killed in the battle for Berlin.

Every day we were expecting to be evacuated to the Americans who were now on the west bank of the River Elbe and had made a historical meeting with the Russians by assembling a pontoon bridge on the River between the two Armies.

The Russians however would not release us until an agreement was made with the Allies to release the same number of prisoners from their side.

What made it more frustrating was the news on the BBC which reported thousands of ex P.O.W.'s were released and on their way home. We must have been the only Camp in Russian hands and they were not going to be flexible about conditions for our release ; it was as though we were hostages again.

The food improved but only to the extent of pork being added to the seaweed soup ; one pig a day was butchered and cooked.

The news on the radio was that the Russians had surrounded Berlin, and Hitler and Eva Braun had committed suicide in a bunker and their bodies burned.

The Russians now held us and had no intention of letting us go, in fact rumours started that we could indeed be held hostage for some sinister motive by them, after all as far as we saw it, they had no respect whatever for their own P.O.W.'s.

A number of Germans, mostly elderly men, who were conscripted into the Army near the end of the War, and survived the carnage around the Camp, were now coming to the Camp to seek protection, but the Russian ex POW's who were on guard outside the gate shot them as they approached, even though their hands were raised. We realised the Russians would show no mercy after the atrocities committed by the Germans in their Country.

Many prisoners fearing their fate in Soviet hands decided to leave the Camp and travel west to the American lines. Several were never seen again.

A Norwegian General the Senior Officer in the Camp who was whisked off in a jeep by the Russians one morning evidently turned up in Moscow and reported to the American Military Mission that the conditions in Luckenwald under the Russians were extremely bad, and the treatment of American and British prisoners was not good.

On looking back at the weeks when we were held by the Russians in Luckenwald I now believe they intended to hold Allied prisoners as hostages, in some quarters, it was thought, to use them to blackmail the Allies into recognising the puppet Communist Government in Poland after the war, and exchange them for Russian prisoners in Allied hands ; one British Airman for 6 Russian soldiers or 3 Officers.

In my opinion I do not think any live prisoners were taken to Russia after the War, and are still there. The Eastern Front in 1945 was a very dangerous place for Allied prisoners who made a run towards the American lines. Russian soldiers were treated worse than animals by their officers and behaved like animals ; some excuse can be made if they retaliated against the Germans, but for anyone to try and travel to freedom through their lines was asking for trouble. Prisoners were dressed in all kinds of clothing and if the Russian soldiers detained any of them they would probably be treated as young German soldiers wearing civilian clothes and shot. This would probably be the reason why they were never heard of again and why so many could not be accounted for.

I know I was frustrated at the Russian attitude and when I saw many of my fellow prisoners making a run for the West was tempted to follow them. Many of them decided to go on the spur of the moment, thinking it would be easy to get through the Russian lines but how wrong they were, and no doubt some paid with their lives.

News eventually came through that the Russians had taken Berlin. The Americans and Russians were on the banks of the River Elbe, and the British were taking the Northern part of Germany and Denmark.

The Armistice to end the European War was to be signed with the unconditional surrender of Nazi Germany on the 8th May 1945.

On that date we were still waiting for the Russians to release us ; but they would not move on their intention to detain us until an exchange was arranged. At that time we were doubtful if any notification of our existence had been made by the Russians to Allied Supreme Headquarters in Rheims.

They did however, improve our accommodation by moving us into the Forelager, an area near the Camp gates which had been the German living and administrative quarters and were very comfortable. When they evacuated the Camp the area was taken over by the French Labour Force.

I was made responsible for bringing soup from the kitchen in a large wooden tub, to the inhabitants of the block every day. It was carried by four men and I served it equally to each rooms representatives who took their share away in containers.

Whilst I was sharing it out a small crowd of foreign labour who were now free, would wait around hoping a small amount of soup would be left in the tub for them. However as they were not recognised by the Russians as Prisoners of War no arrangements were made for them to be supplied with food, and I found myself in an agonising situation, because apart from the soup and a thick slice of brown bread, and mint tea once per day, our subsistence was nil.

I would leave a small amount of soup in the tub and as soon as I turned my back they would fight over it. When we came to take the tub back after our meal, grooves were gouged inside the tubs where the men had scraped their spoons to get every last drop of soup.

Instructions were given to us that we could walk within one mile of the Camp ; and the air raid siren would be sounded if the Russians finally agreed to release us to the Americans, when we should immediately return.

One day an Australian pilot and myself decided to walk into the forest as we thought all pockets of German resistance were cleared up. We reached a point about ¾ mile from the Camp and came across a clearing where a field kitchen had been situated before the Russian breakthrough.

I remember some photographs of German families were scattered around with several German helmets. We picked up one of the helmets and as we did so a voice in English said :-

"Ah ! What have we here ? "

110

On looking round and to our horror stood two German soldiers and a young woman who evidently was a nurse. One of the soldiers held a luger pistol which was pointed at us.

The one who spoke said "Are you English Kriegsgefangenen ? " (P.O.W.'s). We said "yes" and he said "Do you know who we are ? " at the same time opening his tunic under which was a black shirt with yellow skull and crossbones ; The ensignia of the S.S.

He wanted to know if we had food and we told him that although the Russians had taken the Camp they would not release us and provided very little food.

He said with a smile "Probably Britain and America will now fight the Bolsheviks". All the time both of us thought our time had come because they would not let us return to the Camp in case we reported their whereabouts.

It was the worst moment of our captivity ; we had both come through the War after being shot down ; and all the other life threatening experiences, and here we were through our stupidity, walking in a forest where thousands of Germans were killed fighting the Russians, but some of them must have survived and be hiding with nowhere to go.

After studying the situation the German, much to our relief, told us to go back to the Camp and bring back food, I couldn't believe it ; he was letting us go too easily and we would finish up with a bullet in the back when we turned to leave the clearing. Those twenty five steps back to the trees were the longest of my life, we dare not start running, in case he pressed the trigger, but in his mind he probably thought we would help them, especially with a girl to protect.

When we reached the trees we continued walking for a short distance before sprinting back to the Camp.

Our duty was to notify the Senior British Officer in case other men came across the Germans and were not so lucky as we were. He in turn told the Russians who sent out a party to deal with them. The outcome was that one German was killed but the other soldier and the girl had disappeared.

After our escape nobody went back into the forest but moved around the edge of the Camp and walked into Luckenwald. About half a mile from the Camp was a small lake around which were holiday chalets probably owned by Berliners who occupied them at weekends. The furniture and china in some of the chalets had been of a very high quality when left by the owners the previous summer, but the Russians had taken most of them and destroyed the rest ; it made you realise that a victorious army had no scruples when it came to valuable and beautiful items, they were either smashed or taken.

There were signs on the lake that fish were somewhere swimming about and some Russian soldiers decided they would catch some for a meal.

It was a warm day and one or two of the ex prisoners decided to have a swim. They entered the lake and moved a short distance from the edge where the water was deep enough for them. Unfortunately at that moment the Russians 'went fishing' not by normal method but by hand grenades which they threw in the water.

The swimmers made a quick exit and it was a good job they were only a few yards out ; because when the grenades exploded scores of stunned fish rose to the surface to provide the Russians with their meal. No one took a swim again.

I witnessed a very funny scene later in Luckenwald when about two hundred Russian soldiers confiscated bicycles ; some of them had never seen one before, because they rode round and round a field without any control and as they smashed into each other - picked themselves up laughing and mounted the bikes again.

It showed me that something we took for granted in the West ; bicycle riding was not a part of Russian childhood because they had no bicycles.

A couple of weeks after the end of the War a buzz of excitement went through the Camp. A convoy of American Army lorries in charge of a Major, arrived to take as many Allied prisoners as possible to the American lines.

Evidently one of the men who decided to strike out for the River Elbe must have succeeded and informed them of our predicament.

The Americans did not hesitate, they just sent the twenty lorries with instructions to bring back as many of us as possible.

However the Russians were having none of it and ordered the Major to take his lorries back to base. They would not let any of us leave the Camp until agreement was reached between them and the Americans on exchange of prisoners.

It was an unbelievable situation because the War had been over for two weeks.

They also told the American Major that if any attempt was made by us to leave the Camp en masse this would have serious consequences and he would be arrested. Nevertheless secret orders were given by the Camp leaders that at 6am the next day the convoy would be waiting a mile outside the Camp to take us to the American lines.

When morning came everyone was intent on getting out, because of the frustration and depression waiting for the Russians to move us West.

They certainly moved that morning but not the way we wanted ; they placed their soldiers, fully armed, in the areas between the Camp and the lorries and waited for us to appear ; which we did in numbers.

Threats were made that any further advance would result in some of us being hurt ; we recognised that the no nonsense mood they were in any antagonism on our part would lead to them carrying out their threat.

There was nothing more to do but return to Camp even more depressed than before, and the vehicles returned to the American sector.

It was now approaching the end of May and from accounts on the radio all ex Prisoners of War, except us, had been repatriated. Things were getting desperate and our only hope were the people who knew about the Camp, and who were now in the American sector, maybe pressure would be put on the Russians to release us.

One day soon after our attempted escape we had a visit from a well known American War Correspondent called Ed Beattie who was on his way to Berlin to file a report for the 'Stars and Stripes' an American Forces newspaper.

He arrived in a jeep and was very surprised when he was greeted by American and British Commonwealth ex prisoners who informed him of the inflexible attitude taken by the Russians and would he notify General Eisenhower, the Allied Supreme Commander, of the situation.

He said that Allied Headquarters had no idea there were ex prisoners at Luckenwald ; he immediately turned the jeep round to return to the American sector and said he would contact General Eisenhower to obtain our release.

The next morning we knew he had kept his promise because at approximately 11am came the wonderful sound of the Camp air raid siren to summon everyone to the Camp - we were going home !.

In no time at all the Russians provided lorries (Lease Lend from the U.S.A.) to transport us to the Elbe ; but they would not release us until word was received that an equivalent number of their men were waiting at the River to be exchanged.

They must have received the message because we were soon loaded onto Lease Lend lorries and transported to the Elbe. When we arrived a pontoon bridge connected the East and West banks ; this has since been recorded in history books as the place where the armies of East and West finally met to complete the occupation of Germany at the end of the Second World War.

We could not believe the speed at which we were released after the Western Allies heard of the situation at Luckenwald, and lost no time in crossing the bridge to the waiting American lorries. They whisked us off to one of their bases at Halle, where we stayed overnight and enjoyed food which we had forgotten existed.

Chapter 13

Repatriation

The next day we were flown to Brussels and then to England, staying at Bicester for twenty four hours before being taken to Cosford for re-kitting and then home to a tearful reunion.

So ended my time as a Prisoner of War in Germany.

For a short time after returning home I never thought of those months where danger was an everyday companion, but as I gradually blended back into a normal life my mind began to reconstruct the various stages of captivity and what may have happened ; it was then I realised how lucky I had been.

It was bad enough being a Prisoner of War but one had complete faith in the Geneva Convention for protection. However when the tide started to turn against Germany you began to lose confidence as the Nazis showed signs they would not hesitate to eliminate prisoners, especially airmen, who had destroyed their Country's war production and morale of the people.

We could have been the last victims of a tyrannical and cruel regime, probably suffering a similar death to the victims of concentration camps.

Chapter 14

Return to England

After returning to England at the end of May I awaited instructions as to my future role in the War against Japan.

There was talk of Bomber Command attacking the Nippon Empire using Lincoln Bombers which I had not flown.

However the War against Japan ended in August 1945 when the Americans dropped two atoms bombs, one on Hiroshima and the other on Nagasaki which resulted in Japan surrendering unconditionally.

In November I was sent on a refresher course to Coleby Grange near Lincoln, again to fly the Airspeed Oxford. It was 21 months since I had handled the controls of an aircraft but everything came back without any problems.

It was the first time I had flown over a 'lit up' Country and it was a bit confusing getting used to the lights.

One night another pilot and myself were doing circuits and bumps and as I was doing a climbing turn from the flare-path after taking off, noticed the other aircraft on a downwind leg of the circuit with one engine on fire.

The pilot was calling the Control Tower on R.T. but was getting no response. I thought there must be a fault in communication from his aircraft, so I called the Control Tower to report the situation and they acknowledged the message. I circled the airfield as the other pilot approached the flare-path with the engine still on fire, but could see the lights of the Fire Engine as it waited for him to land, which he did successfully.

I then saw the aircraft come to a standstill and in the darkness saw the flames extinguished by the Fire Engine.

It was a lucky escape for the pilot.

In the spring of 1946 I was interviewed at Snaith and had to decide my future in the R.A.F.

I was told that if I wished to continue flying I would be posted to R.A.F. Dishforth, Transport Command, to familiarise myself with the Avro York ; these aircraft were bringing soldiers back from the Far East to England. They were crewed to carry a co-pilot, a position I thought I would fill, but at the interview was told I would be Captain because of my experience with the Lancaster, and an immediate decision was required.

The War had been over for a year and during that time I had recurring nightmares, always finding myself descending without a parachute. For several months I dreaded going to sleep, and with this on my mind an immediate return to flying was out of the question, so I asked to be discharged.

Several bomber pilots transferred to Transport Command and later transferred to B.O.A.C.

Since 1946 I have visited the old airfield at Metheringham three times; the last time for a Squadron Museum day in 1996 when some of my relatives and friends accompanied me.

The Museum was opened by the Family who owned the land on which the airfield was built. They have considerable affection for '106' and always welcome members of the Squadron.

I often recall times when the Lancasters took off for a raid and swept past the Farm near the end of the runway, with wheels raised and locked, engines screaming with extra boost to give pilots a gradual build up of speed before starting to climb with wing tip too near the ground for comfort. The inhabitants of the Farm must have willed the bombers to keep climbing during those tense moments.

In 1996 I stood at the end of the main runway and many thoughts ran through my mind such as taking off and seeing the 'cats eyes' eight hundred yards from the end of the runway, they appeared to be nearer the beginning than the end.

Then the time we returned from Frankfurt with a badly damaged aircraft after a fighter attack, and having to land in darkness on the starboard side of the flarepath where the Lancaster had drifted, and afterwards realising how lucky we were when I saw the damaged aircraft in daylight.

Finally, our final operation - Nuremberg, the futility of it when all the elements were against us and why so many young men perished, including five of my crew, Colin, Johnnie, George, Joe and Jock, for what was 'A Go at whatever cost operation'. This is borne out by the hundreds of headstones in Hanover War Cemetery with the date 30th March 1944 and ages ranging from eighteen to twenty one years.

That is why the aircrew who died will be remembered for their courage, and I pay tribute to the five lads in my Crew for their skill and 'esprit de corps' on the 22 operations we flew together including the 9 to Berlin.

I now appeal to Wally, our Bomb Aimer 'You will have to go round again Skipper' who managed to escape from the blazing Lancaster as she went down. If you read this book you will know I am still around having survived the explosion when she blew up, which no doubt you saw when you 'came down'.

The reason Wally thinks I perished when the Bomber exploded is because he told a Wireless Operator from Barnsley who was in the same Stalag that no one in the aircraft could have survived.

Chapter 15

Return to Germany 1997

It would not have been possible to write this Chapter without the co-operation and prompting of Jonathan who made all the air and transport arrangements for both our visits to Germany in 1997 and 1998.

He is a retired Mining Engineer who, once he is interested in a part of History, will collect and read all the data available or seek information, as in the case of the Nuremberg raid on 30th/31st March 1944, and in particular 'Q' Queenie.

As the Chapter unfolds his tenacity for seeking out details about the Lancaster will reveal some interesting theories both from what happened to the aircraft when it exploded, and the parts which have been salvaged from the wreckage by Herr Reiner Klug and his colleagues of the Herborn Luft War Society.

Even now over fifty years after the action the Society who use metal detectors are finding parts in dense woods which lie in the Konigsberg Area and are convinced there are many more, including one of the Merlin engines, which they hope to locate. Jonathan is in regular communication with them and is gradually building a file and video about 'Q' Queenie.

Our first trip to Germany was made in May 1997 ; we did not have a connection with anyone in Konigsberg so Martin Middlebrooke, Author of 'The Nuremberg Raid', gave me a few names of people who helped him with his research for the book. One was Reiner Klug, who I telephoned and asked if he would be able to meet us at the Village. He told me the Society had always hoped that I, the Pilot of 'Q' Queenie would contact them, to help them with the history of the Lancaster and crew ; he was on holiday during the first two days of our visit but would try and meet me on our last night in Konigsberg.

We flew to Dusseldorf on an early morning flight, picked up a car and travelled to Konigsberg via Cologne, where we had lunch and a stroll round the Cathedral area.

We were surprised, after seeing pictures of the City in ruins, at the change, with an almost new City rising from what had been complete destruction, except for the Cathedral which stood as it had done for centuries with only superficial damage caused by bomb and shell splinters.

From Cologne we estimated the journey to Konigsberg, which had been difficult to pinpoint on the map, would take three hours. It is situated north of Wetzlar and, naturally I was excited and curious to see that small part of Germany where I landed. After fifty years it was as though I was revisiting a place only seen in a dream, or a nightmare, the

Konigsberg village and Berghoff/Reemuhle

View looking towards crash site from hotel 1000 metre distance,
Konigsberg

characters would have changed or passed on and although I had visions
in my minds eye of parts of the Village and countryside, no doubt these
would change after we arrived.

We left Cologne on a late spring afternoon ; the weather was glorious as
we drove on the autobahn south towards Frankfurt. The route to
Nuremberg in March 1944 ran parallel to the autobahn along which
many bombers were shot down. As I watched the traffic speeding along
I thought of the thousands of allied aircraft passing high overhead in
1943/44 and the sounds of their engines receding as they flew to the
target. I remember I never felt as lonely when I hit the ground after
descending by parachute and heard the same sound gradually fade until
only silence and the moon kept me company.

On reaching Wetzlar we experienced some difficulty in hitting the right
road to Konigsberg, which is only a small village about six miles away
and when we asked an inhabitant of Wetzlar, who could speak a little
English, for directions, we were surprised when he said he had never
heard of the place.

We eventually came to a road which ran in the right direction ; there
was no mention of Konigsberg on any sign post and after climbing

sensed, from my brief stay in 1944, was very near the village and after travelling a few hundred yards we came to a sign post pointing to Konigsberg, which we could see about ¼ mile down the road.

At this point I wondered if I would recognise any part of the Village, but as the first building on the outskirts was an hotel, the Berghoff/Reemuhle, we decided, if it was suitable to book in for a couple of nights.

The Proprietor Gretel Reeh who spoke good English when told of our mission was very interested but said she was not local to the area and had no knowledge of what happened to the Village during the War.

After booking in, our next step was to trace anyone who lived in the Village in 1944, so we decided to have a walk round and make enquiries. We soon realised how pretty it was, the hotel was situated on a road which ran through the Village, and the rest of the streets which are very narrow, rose steeply to the brow of a hill on top of which stood the Schoolmaster's large house dominating the skyline. Most of the timbered houses were very old, probably 17th Century, but a lot of the Village had been built since the War, and the villas were eye-catching with their colourful gardens and hanging baskets making them even more attractive.

It was very quiet as we strolled around, and those people who we saw were too young to have lived during the War. However I encountered one young man and told him who I was 'the Pilot of a Lancaster bomber which crashed near the Village in 1944' and could he advise me of any old resident who may remember the incident. He spoke good English and surprised me when he said the incident had been talked about since the War and the man I should contact was Herr Lepper, a shoemaker who still lived in the Village. We continued our walk hoping to find someone who knew Herr Lepper and as we went along, a lady in her 60's who was working in her garden heard us mention the name whereupon she said "Ja" nodding her head and pointed to a villa at the corner of a street fifty yards away.

We walked to the door, to start what was going to be a very interesting and informative two days, pressed the communication buzzer to which a lady answered. I told her who I was 'Pilot Luft crash 1944' and she immediately opened the door, no doubt wondering what I looked like after all the years. The last time, when she was a young girl of fourteen, I was lying on a stretcher in the Burgermeister's Office, severely injured. I was also a little apprehensive of my reception as a wartime flyer who had helped to destroy her Country. However I had no need to worry because with a curious smile she welcomed me and informed the lady in the garden who I was, who also smiled and waved her hand.

The lady was Frau Lepper who invited us into the house ; she opened the curtains in the lounge to reveal a panoramic view across the valley, and pointed to where the Lancaster crashed. She was our first witness to the crash and it was a stroke of luck finding her. She was fourteen in

Standing in front of the field where "Q" Queenie crashed

The spot where I landed and made an impression in the Earth

March 1944, and on the night of the Nuremberg Raid, due to the aerial activity of bombers flying towards the East and anti aircraft fire, she was looking to see what was happening, when she saw 'Q' Queenie spinning down like a falling leaf on fire to crash and explode at the far side of a wood.

We told her we were planning to spend two days in Konigsberg, thanked her for helping us and returned to the Berghoff for a meal.

On arriving back to the hotel, I looked out of the window in Jonathan's room which faced open country, where a cart track ran from the back of the building to disappear over a hill about ¾ mile away. Although it was the first time I had returned to the Village I had a feeling of travelling on the track before, it was as though I had walked on it to get to a certain place but never arrived.

After we went into the bar for a drink the door opened and a fresh faced grey haired man walked in and talked to Gretel who quickly introduced us to Herr Irwin Lepper.

The next two minutes were electric. Gretel translated for us and gave us the news that when I lay badly injured near the wood in 1944 Irwin Lepper was a boy of fourteen and he found me after I called "Help Englander" I remember this was after seeing a torch light in the distance.

A search party had appeared some two hours after the crash when they found four of the crew dead and Irwin heard me shouting. When I heard this news I was elated and gave him a big 'thank you'.

He then made a sign for us to follow him, and went outside, we took him to the car because we had an idea he was going to take us to the crash site. The car was parked at the back of the hotel and he directed Jonathan to proceed along the cart track I had seen from the window. We drove to the hill and after about a further two hundred yards he signalled for us to get out and then walked fifty yards before stopping at a field of approximately three acres.

Irwin pointed to the far side and indicated it was the area where the Lancaster crashed and exploded breaking into three pieces making a crater seventeen yards long and six yards deep with one of the engines landing in the next field. There was a slight dip in the ground where it crashed and Jonathan, who studied rock strata, said the many pieces of rock still scattered around would have been blasted from a depth of about 20'.

This part of our journey was traumatic for me because it was the first time I had seen that part of Germany, where I had landed with such force amongst the blazing wreckage with the bodies of four lads from my crew lying within 150 metres of where I lay. Even after all that time, on a beautiful sunny spring evening, so quiet with only the birds singing their nightly chorus in my ears, I thought of the crew who were so near finishing their operational tour, only to be sacrificed on a mission which should never have got off the ground.

With Irwin, Lina Lepper and daughter in law Sylvia

View of Konisgsberg village from crash site

It was astounding the way things had gone ; within two hours of arriving in Konigsberg, we had met a person who saw the Lancaster crash and explode and been shown the crash site and the spot where I was located by the man who was now with us in the German countryside. It was a completely unexpected scenario.

We spent some time at the crash site before returning to the Berghoff for dinner and arranging to see Irwin the next day. When we entered the dining room for our evening meal Jonathan struck up a conversation with a German couple in their 60's ; the man spoke good English. Jonathan told them the object of our visit and they showed great interest. He went on to describe the destruction of the Lancaster and my miraculous escape, he had brought Martin Middlebrooke's book 'The Nuremberg Raid' with him which he passed to the gentleman to browse through at dinner, but he was so fascinated with the operation he read some of it whilst he was eating, and then asked me questions. What surprised him was the large number of R.A.F. Bombers operating over German Cities at one time.

The lady who serves breakfast at the Berghoff is sixty eight years of age and owns a 'ranch' as she calls it adjacent to the hotel where she breeds horses for a hobby.

On the night of 30th/31st March 1944 she was fourteen years of age living on the ranch with her family, and in good English told us that three bombs fell from the aircraft and exploded in the woods at the bottom of their property some 100 yds from the crash site.

The next day, Saturday, we again visited the site, the weather was glorious which allowed us to have a good look round and for Jonathan to take photographs. We walked along the rows of green corn for fifteen minutes or so when I noticed a piece of perspex about 1½" in length which appeared to be a switch handle cover (This was later identified as a switch cover from the Navigator's G set).

We then left this quiet part of the countryside and drove down a short distance to the beautiful City of Wetzlar where I had been taken to a Lazarett by horse and cart following my capture earlier in the morning of 30th/31st March 1944.

I wanted to identify the building where I was treated.

Wetzlar is a small beautiful City with a Cathedral, a river running through it, and the architecture is quaint and very interesting. It would appear to be a place with plenty of commerce and in summer attracts many visitors. The Cathedral is situated in the old part where there are many shops and narrow streets, and is reached by walking up a hill for approximately ¼ mile. We were looking for the Information Centre which we found in the square opposite the Cathedral. A Czech lady, married to a German, was on duty and was very helpful. After we told her of our quest she telephoned someone who evidently knew all about wartime Wetzlar because she was then able to tell us where the place we were looking for was situated. A bank had been constructed on the site 18 months ago, but the building I remember as a Lazarett was a school before and after the War, when it was demolished to make way for the bank. On looking at the map our route out of the City passed the bank which was a large and splendid building ; It was by far another time when I had been taken there by horse and cart.

Incidentally, 'Q' Queenie was attacked by the Me 110 night fighter over Wetzlar. From Wetzlar we drove to Geissen, some 10km east of the City. This was where I started my journey by rail in a cattle truck to Oberhausel near Frankfurt for interrogation after I was shot down and where I first saw the trappings of a police state ; apart from the Wermach and Luftwaffe uniforms there were many more from branches of the security forces of the Third Reich.

We were invited to the Leppers on Saturday evening and what a pleasant and hospitable night we had, although Dr. Herman Lepper, their son, was away at a conference, his young wife Sylvia who is a pharmacist and spoke excellent English, came to the house, to help us with our communication. I gave them a detailed account of what happened to the aircraft in the skies over their village on 30th/31st March 1944. I told them how many crew members there were and that six of us were in the aircraft when the petrol tanks exploded at 18000 ft ; the Bomb Aimer already having bailed out. I said I had not been able to locate him since the War but we were again making enquiries and hoped to be successful.

They were also surprised when I told them how many bombers, 800, were operating over Germany that night. After their surprise and also the same reaction by the German in the dining room of the Berghoff it made me wonder if Herman Gorings prediction that not one enemy bomber would fly over Germany, and the subsequent large numbers of allied bombers that did, if their propaganda machine tried to soften the obvious by admitting only a few planes had penetrated German airspace.

I was also told by the Leppers that the blast from the bombs and the aircraft crashing 1000 metres from the village caused some damage to houses which had walls and windows blown out. When we visited the crash site and looked back at the village the 1000 metres seemed only a stones throw away. If the aircraft had crashed on it the 4,000lb bomb would have wiped Konigsberg off the map and killed all the inhabitants.

It is indeed remarkable that on returning to the village after fifty three years the eye witnesses to the crash Lina and Irwin, who found me, had married and we came together in their village to complete the story of what had been a terrifying experience for all of us.

It was an interesting and absorbing evening we spent with them and Sylvia and one which we will never forget.

The following day, Sunday, we visited the local cemetery where five of my crew were buried after the crash, but their remains were later taken by the War Graves Commission to Hanover and placed in the cemetery, a place we were to visit before our return home.

Afterwards we called on Irwin and Lina to say farewell before leaving Konigsberg for Meiningen and Obermassfeld some 150 miles from Wetzlar where I was hospitalised for four months.

We drove through beautiful countryside and after calling for lunch carried on; after climbing a long rise we saw what appeared to be an aerodrome control tower on the hill in front of us. However, as we approached the structure, which was very tall, we realised we were crossing the old border into what had been East Germany and the structure was a watch tower that had been manned by the East German Army. As far as the eye could see to the north the forest had been felled to make a wide corridor where rolls of barbed wire fences were erected.

As soon as we passed the tower the road ran downhill to Meiningen and when we passed through the first village what caught our eye was the lack of maintenance to property and roads. Houses had not been painted for years and woodwork was rotting, even the gardens were overgrown and the road surfaces were wilfully neglected. No wonder the rivers were polluted and affected people's health, they also had an air of poverty about them.

When we entered Meiningen which I remember from what little I saw of it fifty three years ago was a beautiful town, like an English spa town, with large and magnificent buildings. It was one of these buildings, a concert hall, which was part of a complex of wonderful architecture which had been used as a hospital for injured P.O.W.'s.

The grounds of the theatre were circled by a barbed wire fence with more open ground, like a small park on the other side and a narrow river of clear water running through it.

It was hard to believe this was the same place, all the grass and weeds were overgrown, making the area seem smaller than it did in 1944. It would have been interesting to have entered the building which was locked, and seen the auditorium, which was a dormitory for scores of prisoners, and also the rehearsal room where I slept and the American Infantry Officer related his experience on the night that 'Mars invaded the USA'.

From Meiningen we drove the few miles to Obermassfeld which is still a pretty place because it is too small to notice any neglect.

The building where I was held had been an Agricultural College pre war and is now converted to an Administrative Block for Agriculture.

The village still has the 'Pinochio' scenario and as we walked round the outside of the building I pointed out to Jonathan the dormitory where I stayed with other aircrew, R.A.F. and U.S.A.A.F.

I recalled the old days especially May Day in 1944 when after being given parole we hobbled on crutches or in plastercasts to the river bank at the rear of the building where we sat near a lake, now much smaller and overgrown with weeds, to watch a softball match between 'the legless and armless', there were many amputees at Obermassfeld.

It was here at Obermassfeld where Group Captain Massie, en route for repatriation from Stalag Luft III, gave an emotional account of the mass murder of the 50 R.A.F. Officers who escaped from the camp and were shot on recapture.

He notified Anthony Eden, the Foreign Secretary, of the massacre on his arrival in Britain, and after the War those responsible were caught and executed or received long prison sentences.

Jonathan took some photographs before we set off north for Hanover on the North German Plain some 180 miles away. We made a few good miles before evening then felt it would be beneficial to us if we stopped somewhere and stayed overnight. This we did and booked in at an old 16th Century Berghoff in the village Fisvald, still in what was East Germany.

We enjoyed a good meal and had a long discussion with two young men, one a joiner, the other a long distance lorry driver. We asked them about the old East Germany and how the new Germany was affecting their way of living. They told us it was good to have free speech, it would not have been possible under the old regime to have talked to us in such a way. They were also able to make more money which was helping their standard of living.

After breakfast on the last day, Monday, we travelled by autobahn to Hanover. We needed to locate the British War Graves Cemetery and called at a travel agents for directions, they advised us to ask at the Information Centre in the main railway station about ½ mile away.

I could never have negotiated the traffic which Jonathan had to face to get there. It seemed that Central Hanover was the object of a major traffic changeover, the disorganisation and traffic problems were chaotic with overpasses, underpasses, trams and traffic lights, they mixed the lot.

We eventually arrived at the main parking area at the front of the station and Jonathan went to the Information Centre where he was given a map with directions how to get to the area where the Cemetery was situated. What they did not tell him was that due to motorway renewals we could not get to the Cemetary as directed. Whilst he was away I was watching people going in and out of the station and remembered the last time I was there ; it was in a Lancaster at 21,000ft and the station was our aiming point ; so I was probably sitting in an area where buildings were destroyed by our H.E. and incendiary bombs ; talk about a funny feeling.

We eventually reached the West side of Hanover and found the Cemetery in a peaceful country area.

For me this was the difficult part of our visit ; it was so quiet as we entered the Cemetery in the early evening sunlight and I was struck with extreme sorrow as I looked upon row after row of headstones and could not imagine the boys of Bomber Command lying there ; I could only see them as they prepared for another operation. I could not believe their broken and shattered bodies had been taken from the ground where they crashed to be put in the graves in front of me ; I was wishing them back to tap me on the shoulder and say "I am here, not down there".

After talking to the German Gardener on duty we perused the Roll of Honour kept in book form and found the names and plots where the five lads of my crew lay, all of them in separate graves in the front row about 50 yds from the road.

I looked at the headstones on the graves of Colin, Johnny, George, Jock and Joe and said a prayer for them. I thought of the last time we stood by the Lancaster before taking off for Nuremberg. The quietness surrounding the airfield that night was so intense that you could hear the silence ; the air was frosty under a clear full moon, which in 2½ hours time would light up the condensation trails made by our aircraft and aid the night fighter to destroy us, shortening the lives of five young men with whom I had shared life for such a short time 53 years ago.

I had been their Captain and Pilot through 22 operational trips, we had been shot at by night fighters and anti aircraft guns, faced 600 searchlights over Berlin and 1,200 guns, and even the weather which

The graves of Joe, Johnnie, Colin, George and Jock. Hanover War Cemetery. 1997

was treacherous through the winter of 1943/44 had tried to destroy us by icing up the pitot head and robbing us of the air speed indicator on our first trip.

I was very upset and Jonathan could see how it had affected me, he had an idea it would be stressful so had brought a 'tot' to toast the five lads and all the other aircrew laid to rest in the Cemetery.

As we left the Cemetery I looked back at the five headstones and could feel their eyes on me with their voices telling me they were ready for 'take off '.

I quietly closed the gates and walked to the car.

Here I have to write about Joe Ellick the Rear Gunner. Joe was a Jew and came from Wallasey. Since the War we have heard about the Holocaust and Hitler's plan to eradicate the Jews. Joe volunteered for aircrew and sadly he was killed but if he had survived there would have been no protection for him under the Geneva Convention or a place in a P.O.W. Camp. The Germans would have quickly identified him as a Jew and would have transferred him to a concentration camp where all traces of him would have disappeared. It is a frightening thought when a young man who volunteered for aircrew without much chance for survival, would in all probability have been murdered in a concentration camp because he was a Jew. There was no way he could have survived the War.

Before I left the Cemetery I made copies of the epitaphs on three of the graves which are set out below :

JOHNNIE
God took you Johnnie it was his will
Why so soon we wonder still
Till we meet

JOCK
God gained ; we lost
But they are not dead
Who live in the hearts of others

JOE
God gave us strength
to bear the loss
What it cost to lose him
No one will ever know

When I spoke to Reiner Klug by telephone on our return he told me he went to the War Cemetery the day after, and the attendants confirmed our visit.

It was a sad end to four very interesting days. I had gone to Germany hoping to meet people from Konigsberg who remembered the

Chapter 16

Germany revisited 1998

I decided to return to Germany for a second time in May 1998 when Jonathan and Jean, his wife, arranged a holiday to coincide with the visit. We were to fly from Manchester to Frankfurt, pick up a car at the airport and travel to Konigsberg, approximately fifty miles distance, stay at the hotel for three nights after which they would bring me back to Frankfurt for the return flight to Manchester, and then continue their holiday touring the Black Forest and Southern Germany.

Jean was looking forward to the visit after our stay the previous year where we established a good relationship with the inhabitants of Konigsberg.

After collecting the car, a black ford Mondeo Estate, at the airport, we drove to Oberhausel so I could have a look at the site of Dulag Luft. After my stay there in 1944 it was bombed ; and R.A.F. aircrew were taken to the new Dulag Luft at Wetzlar, but we could not find the site, and after several enquiries no one could help us because they had never heard of the place. From Oberhausel we travelled to Geissen Station where I wanted to show them the platform where an Australian Flight

Jean and I watching an incendiary bomb from "Q" Queenie being dug up at Konigsberg.

Remains of incendiary bomb uncovered at Konigsberg

Lieutenant was punched to the ground by a German Stormtrooper in khaki uniform, with swastika armband, as we waited for the train to take us to Dulag Luft.

I easily recognised the platform, even though the station was bombed and destroyed near the end of the War. It had been rebuilt with the same number of platforms. What a difference to the place compared to 1944 when I felt utterly broken as I lay on the platform severely injured. It was probably shock after being shot down two days previously, but seeing all the servicemen and other Nazi uniforms was so depressing to me, the future appeared hopeless.

Now on a cheerful and bright afternoon, it seemed as though Hitler and his rotten regime had never existed ; and the Germans I saw on the station would probably accept he was part of their history which could not be erased but put him out of their minds and carry on with their lives.

After our description of the last visit to Konigsberg Jean was keen to go there to visit the crash site, so we left Geissan and arrived at the Berghoff approximately thirty minutes later.

The hotel was closed for the afternoon, so we immediately went to the site. The place has a quiet atmosphere similar to that of going into a Cathedral, and you find yourselves talking in hushed tones ; and I also find it difficult to think of the plane crashing but remember four of the crew lying dead very near where I landed and that fills me with sadness at the way they were suddenly taken, all within less than twenty seconds.

I think we were all a little overcome by the visit, thinking of the Lancaster coming down a mass of flames and exploding as it hit the ground. It is a place which still has a hold on me because to me it is a part of Germany I feel belongs to the crew.

We returned to the Berghoff where Gretel greeted us, gave us the keys to our rooms where we unpacked and went down for dinner.

131

Bergermeisters office, Konigsberg. Which was the office in 1944 where I was held, severely wounded after being shot down at Konigsberg

Rainier Klug who we had arranged to meet arrived with two friends, I know one was called Claudio but I am not sure of the name of the other gentleman, all three were very pleasant and warmly greeted us. They told me they had something special to show me, and we drove in three cars on the same track towards the crash site before turning down a lane to the right into a valley between two forests on either side.

After alighting from the cars they led us up a wood, which rose steeply to the right ; and stopped after approximately 75 yards where the two younger men commenced digging by the stump of a tree ; after going down about a metre they uncovered a metal object ; it was a 50lb incendiary bomb, an oil filled type from Queenie which had been buried for over fifty years. What an experience for me to see a bomb which amongst others I had last seen in the bomb bay before we set off for Nuremberg fifty years ago.

Six weeks after our visit Rainier Klug posted a brass detonator from the bomb which had been cleaned and renovated by Claudio, which I have placed on the mantelpiece. They also produced a box in which were several small parts of the aircraft one of which was a piece of perspex, 3" square.

We brought the box back with us to England and since then Jonathan had used a magnifying glass to examine it and established it was part of the cover for the H2s scanner. One of the sides of the glass is jagged, and two weeks after first examining the piece he was amazed to notice that on the broken edge was part of a circle exactly 20mm diameter, no doubt caused by a cannon shell.

Get together at Irwin Leppers home 1998 with friends who picked me up in war !

To go back to the destruction of 'Q' Queenie earlier in the story, when I gave the order to bail out all the crew responded over the R.T. except the Wireless operator and Mid Upper Gunner, and as the fighter fired cannon and machine gun from the port quarter down I thought they were both killed when the aircraft was hit. The finding of the piece of perspex with a hole made by a cannon shell would appear to confirm that Jock was killed by the burst from the cannon and machine gun.

When we left the wood to return to the Berghoff for a drink we were absolutely thrilled at the way our second visit was also turning out ; every hour was rewarding as some pieces of 'Q' Queenie were revealed to us which time could not destroy, and we knew there would be more pieces to be found.

The Herborn Luft Society had certainly got their teeth into the search for as many parts of the aircraft they could locate, and were quietly confident that one of the engines would be discovered in the near future.

It had been a very good day for me and that night we had a convivial evening with Reiner Klug, his two friends, Irwin and Lena Lepper, their friends Lina and Verma Reinhardt and Herbert Griebel. Rainier translated both languages for us and the Leppers and after a few drinks we all knew more about the action both in the air and on the ground on the night of 30th/31st March 1944.

On the next day, Saturday, Irwin Lepper and one of his friends drove us to Herborn to meet Reiner and his two friends ; Claudio has a keen sense of humour and served in the German Paratroops Regiment after the War, he is about forty years of age. We had only met them for the first time the previous night when they extricated the oil bomb and they were three very sociable people. They were involved in searching for the remains of 'Q' Queenie over several years and had been successful in their work. They said it excited them when they detected a metal object underground, especially if it was part of the bomber, but the icing on the cake for them was contacting me the Pilot after fifty years.

Jonathan and I realised how lucky we were that these gentlemen 'bent over backwards' to give us all the help possible to try and finalise how 'Q' Queenie was destroyed and what happened to it when it hit the ground and was scattered over many acres.

Reiner and his two comrades were keen to show us the Herborn Air Museum which contained hundreds of parts from shot down R.A.F. and U.S.A.A.F. aircraft. They had gained a great deal of knowledge about allied bombers and had some very interesting stories to tell about their destruction.

One case was almost unbelievable, it was the story of a Flying Fortress which was attacked and damaged on a daylight raid to Leipzig. One of the gunners was killed by the fighter and the pilot and co-pilot could not save the plane which was badly damaged so the order to bale out was given to the crew. The story can be confirmed because there is a photograph of the Flying Fortress which 'belly' landed in the snow in the Herborn area having stayed in the air without a crew for 150 kms before making a 'wheels up landing'. When the Germans looked in the aircraft, expecting to find someone alive, the only occupant was the dead gunner, and of course the cockpit was empty. This absolutely astounded them until all the facts came together after the crew were picked up ; and they in turn were flabbergasted when told how and where the aircraft had landed, after flying 150 kms without anyone at the controls.

Reiner also told us of an American airman with whom he had been in contact; this flyer could remember the location where he landed by parachute because it was a signposted crossroad with names and directions still embedded in his mind. Although it seemed an impossible task to identify this crossroad, Reiner set about the task and eventually did find it. I found him a very interesting man with a nose for searching out the answers to some intriguing questions on man and the machines in which they were shot down over his part of Germany. He told me the American flyer and two of his crew would be at Obermassfeld the same time as I was.

The Museum which is situated in Herborn University houses many parts from shot down allied aircraft which operated in thousands over Germany, and from the statistics of Bomber Command aircrew lost -

55,000 ; it means around 8,000 R.A.F. aircraft were destroyed and many parts salvaged from the wreckage were placed in various museums throughout the Country. In fact the Herborn Society have so many parts they have stored them in several garages.

Reiner Klug and his fellow members of the Society have certainly done a marvellous job with their Museum, we also found them very willing to give us details of their findings on my aircraft, and as I pointed out they waited until our arrival so we could watch them excavate the oil bomb.

After we left the Air Museum a photographer from the local paper arrived and took pictures of our party.

The morning had passed very quickly as we looked around the Museum and it was time for lunch. Reiner had arranged for me to meet the Luftwaffe pilot, Martin Becker, who shot our plane down on the Nuremberg Raid. He is a very sick old man of eighty three but when Rainier telephoned his wife she said that he would be pleased to see me. So I was going to meet the Luftwaffe pilot who destroyed 'Q' Queenie, it was an occasion I never thought would happen. When tracer bullets are hitting the aircraft and flashing past the cockpit window, followed by a fire in the wing and in one of the engines you do not think the man who has fired the weapons is only about 100 yds behind you. At the time you are his target and he may not be doing it for the Fatherland and Hitler but for his family who could be under the falling bombs when the target was attacked thirty minutes later.

Now fifty years on I did not know what his reaction would be at meeting one of the pilots ; he had shot down well over fifty aircraft. It was all part of history and I had no ill feeling towards this man whose ammunition had killed five of my crew.

Martin Becker lives with his wife, who looks after him, in an 18th Century farmhouse in Limbourg. As I said he is very sick and frail who is confined to bed most of the time, but also uses a wheelchair. He greeted me warmly and I immediately thought what a fantastic night fighter pilot he must have been with all those victories, including eight on the Nuremberg raid.

Reiner Klug was present and translated our conversation. Martin said, like a lot more Luftwaffe pilots I had met, it was always their hope that the machine was destroyed and not all the men in it but he knew this was not possible.

Frau Becker also showed me letters and commendations signed by Hitler and Goring. I asked him about the pilots of the Gruppe he commanded ; he told me they enjoyed life whilst they could and were amongst the best pilots in the Luftwaffe. Their attitude to what may be a short life was exactly like the boys on our squadron and here we were Martin Becker and myself on either side of the fence, who could have (did have in his case) brought about the conclusion of my comrades young lives and fears.

135

I left him with a sadness, first of all because I would not see him again, and secondly because he was so ill and frail ; but what a pilot he must have been in his career with the Luftwaffe which he joined in 1936.

The evening was spent as guests of Irwin and Lina Lepper at their house, Herbert Griebel, Virma Reinhardt who were with the search party which found me on 30th/31st March 1944, Lina, Virma's Wife, Dr. Herman Lepper, their son and his wife Sylvia were also there.

We had a most enjoyable night, communication between us was good because of Herman and Sylvias' excellent English and a lot of information was exchanged. A reporter for three daily papers in the Wetzlar, Herborn and Geissan areas was also present and recorded the story of my arrival in Konigsberg by parachute in 1944. This was given by Irwin and his colleagues and must have been quite lengthy because I received copies of the interviews together with photographs when I returned to England ; they would have covered two full pages of an English tabloid newspaper.

They remembered how, as young boys, hearing the droning of engines mingled with the firing of machine guns and cannon from aerial combats between the bombers and German night fighters in one of the fiercest air battles of the War. In the 'Dill District' six bombers fell blazing from the sky and other aircraft went down near Hohenroth, Guntersdorf, Mademuhlen and Haiern ; more crashed in the area near Dotzlar, Cleeborg, Helbs, Bilkheim, Quotshasen, Munchholzhauren, Hachenburg, Berghausen and Konigsberg ('Q' Queenie).

On Sunday, the third day of our visit, arrangements were made for me to visit Herman Schupp with one arm who guarded me in the Bergermeister's Office for twenty four hours before escorting me by horse and cart driven by a member of the Luftwaffe to a Lazarett in Wetzlar.

He is now eighty two years of age, has Alzeimers Disease ; and is looked after by his wife. It is an illness I am familiar with because my Wife, Jean has suffered from it for twelve years and is now in Residential Care.

When I saw him after fifty four years and held his hand while I stroked his face he tightened his grip ; looked me in the eyes as though he remembered what happened all those years ago.

Dr. Herman Lepper and Irwin, his Father, accompanied us to see him and in conversation with Frau Schupp she made an astonishing revelation about what she had seen at the site the morning after the Lancaster crashed.

She said there was a depression 2½" deep in the shape of my body with arms outstretched where I hit the ground at the edge of a wood. I must have landed on my back, rolled over and over and then lapsed into unconsciousness.

At this point of our two visits I had met all the main characters on the German side who were involved with my destiny on 30th/31st March

1944. I would never have believed in the fifty four years since the War ended that this would happen.

After dinner on the last night we discussed the outcome of our visit which had been both surprising and more than interesting. Every hour was filled with information about the bomber and what might be revealed in the future. Jean had been moved when shown the site of the crash and the spot where I landed, with four of the crew lying dead within 150yds of me ; it was all very poignant but said she wouldn't have missed the opportunity to come and also meet some of the people of Konigsberg who found me lying 1,000 metres from the Village.

Whilst we were talking a telephone call came from a young man named Martin Best. He said he had not been aware of my previous visit until I left the district, and had a canvas bag containing parts of the aircraft found over the years on his family's land, which he would be pleased to hand over to me.

I immediately invited him to the hotel and for the next three hours had a most revealing and interesting conversation. He spoke excellent English and now owned the family ranch and riding school near Konigsberg.

Apart from the items in the bag which were small with some of them identifiable, he told me his Mother had found a piece of green leather, approximately 3' square, shortly after the crash. I suppose footwear was scarce in Germany during the War so she had the leather made into a pair of calf length boots which lasted many years. This leather was part of a cushion from my seat in the Lancaster ; I remember the occasion it was placed there by the ground crew who on receiving my request for a cushion immediately took it from the Flight Commander's aircraft, who they did not like. Incidentally he was shot down and killed after we 'bought it'.

I was constantly being surprised by findings and information about things relative to the crash, but the final revelation was that the control column was found by a local man who had recently left the district but it was hoped he would be contacted for the return of the column sometime in the near future.

Meeting this young man Martin, put the icing on the cake of our stay and we agreed to see each other again on my next visit.

On Monday, the last day of my visit, Jonathan drove to Coblenz where there is a museum housing a collection of military equipment including the famous 88mm artillery, anti aircraft and anti tank gun, a most awesome weapon in the Second World War which shot down thousands of allied bombers. There were 1,200 of these guns in flak towers and on the ground in and around Berlin during the Air Battle of that City, and in co-operation with 600 searchlights, one of which is also in the museum, were deadly when throwing up a box barrage at the rate of an ammunition dump every two minutes which seemed to cover every square yard of the sky with bursting shells. The searchlights used by the

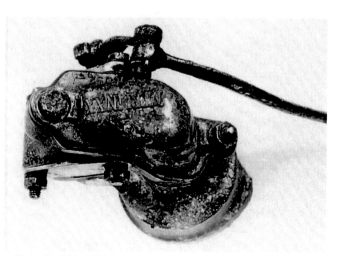

*Part of Merlin XX engine
from "Q" Queenie*

*Above. Detonator from
incendiary dug up in 1998.
Right. Part of perspex
covering H2S scanner and
20mm hole made by cannon.
Thought to be from a burst
that killed Jock & George*

138

Claude and his colleague digging up the incendiary bomb 1998.

*Geissen railway station showing the platform where a German
Stormtrooper knocked down an Australian F/Lt whilst we were waiting for
a train to take us to Dulag Luft.*

Konigsberg Cemetery showing the area where Colin, Johnnie, George, Jock and joe were initially laid to rest.

The famous "88" at Koblenz museum.

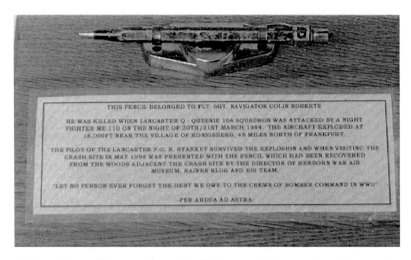

THIS PENCIL BELONGED TO FLT. SGT. NAVIGATOR COLIN ROBERTS

HE WAS KILLED WHEN LANCASTER Q - QUEENIE 106 SQUADRON WAS ATTACKED BY A NIGHT
FIGHTER ME 110 ON THE NIGHT OF 30TH/31ST MARCH 1944. THE AIRCRAFT EXPLODED AT
18,000FT NEAR THE VILLAGE OF KONIGSBERG, 45 MILES NORTH OF FRANKFURT.

THE PILOT OF THE LANCASTER P.O. R. STARKEY SURVIVED THE EXPLOSION AND WHEN VISITING THE
CRASH SITE IN MAY 1998 WAS PRESENTED WITH THE PENCIL WHICH HAD BEEN RECOVERED
FROM THE WOODS ADJACENT THE CRASH SITE BY THE DIRECTOR OF HERBORN WAR AIR
MUSEUM, RAINER KLUG AND HIS TEAM.

"LET NO PERSON EVER FORGET THE DEBT WE OWE TO THE CREWS OF BOMBER COMMAND IN WWII"

-PER ARDUA AD ASTRA-

*Photo of propelling pencil used by Colin, our Navigator, found in woods
in 1998*

*With Jonathan and Jean outside the Herborn Air Museum together with
our German friends*

ABGESCHOSSENER RAF-BOMBERPILOT IN HERBORN AUF SPURENSUCHE

Nachdem seine Lancaster in der Luft explodiert war, kam Richard Starkey erst wieder am geöffneten Fallschirm zu sich

Nur zwei der sieben Besatzungsmitglieder überlebten – In der Nacht zum 31. März 1944 fielen über dem alten Dillkreis sechs Vier-Mots vom Himmel

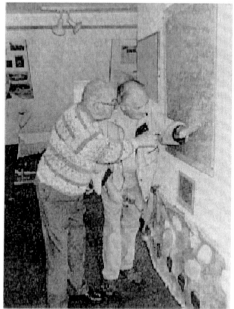

Above. Headlines from German daily newspaper reporting my visit in 1998.

Left. With Reiner examining maps in the Herborn Air War Museum.

Germans were massive with a diameter of two metres and stood about 15' high on their support.

It was the first time I had seen these two implements of war, one to search you out, and the other to destroy you, and when I looked at them, now silent and blind, my mouth went dry the same as it did over Berlin those many years ago.

At this point of my story as I write about the weapons used to destroy allied aircraft my thoughts return to the parachute descent in 1944.

Over the years I have often wondered what effect a burnt parachute attached to the harness by one hook had on the speed of descent.

We have tried to estimate this, and as the normal descent with a whole parachute is 20ft per second my landing would have been at a far higher rate.

To try and solve the question and whilst recently attending a Squadron reunion dinner at Woodhall Spa, I telephoned the Parachute Section at nearby Coningsby R.A.F. Station and explained my problem to Sgt. Williams the N.C.O. in charge. He was very interested and invited me and Jonathan, who was my guest at the dinner, to call at an arranged time the next day when he would have had time to study the question.

We found him very helpful and he had a wartime chest type parachute on display for us together with some literature. After discussing my descent into Germany he said he could not give a definite answer to the question of what effect the condition of the parachute would have on the speed at which I hit the ground, but it would probably have been higher than a normal landing ; and he was also of the opinion that the parachute would be fully open.

I thanked him for his time and the help he had given me.

I knew the severe injuries I received were caused by a very heavy landing at the end of an abnormal descent and over the next few months gave the matter a lot of thought.

I finally decided to go straight to the source of parachute manufacture - Irving - Great Britain Ltd, whose equipment saved thousands of lives in the Second World War and initiated 'The Caterpillar Club' of which I am a member.

The gentleman I contacted was Mr. Cowley who is involved with the testing of parachutes.

After submitting the problem to him and giving him full details of the condition of the parachute on my descent, i.e. attached to the harness by one hook, and hundreds of small holes burnt in it, he said I had clipped it to the harness upside down which would cause the parachute to oscillate on the way down to an angle of approximately 30° to the perpendicular and this could have been increased by the holes.

Incidentally because I was unconscious after being blown out of the Lancaster when it exploded, I had no idea as to what specifically had made the holes. However during the course of writing my story I came up with a possible explanation.

143

The final destruction of the aircraft was caused by the petrol tanks in the port mainplane exploding as the fire reached them causing the wing to break into thousands of pieces of all sizes. Hundreds of these pieces would have been hurled far up into the sky as the aircraft disintegrated, and as they came down, by which time the parachute would have opened with my unconscious body suspended in the harness, it would have been peppered with small pieces of hot metal approximately ½" in size raining down, I estimated the size of the holes by the brilliant moonlight when I regained consciousness and held on to the one attachment.

Sgt. Williams at Coningsby did advise me the reason the hot metal pieces did not set fire to the canopy was because the parachute was made of silk, but I would not have been so lucky with the nylon material used these days, which would have been set alight.

To return to my landing, as I made an impression in the ground over 2" deep it looks as though, with the parachute oscillating, I hit the ground with my back at the bottom of a 'swing'.

After speaking to Mr. Cowley I was able to conclude with some satisfaction how the parachute performed when it brought me safely to earth, but I shall never know how it opened. I do know however that a couple of seconds delay in attaching one hook of the harness to the chute would have resulted in my being blown out of the Lancaster without one.

Apart from Mr.Cowley's expertise in helping me to understand what might have happened after I was blown out of the aircraft, which in itself was a miracle, another remarkable coincidence occurred when I applied to the Caterpillar Club for a replacement pin many years after the War.

I completed an application form giving all details of the parachute descent, together with names of my Crew, five of whom were killed, including Johnnie Harris, the Flight Engineer, and sent it to the Secretary.

On receiving the application the lady telephoned me and said she had read all the details with interest, including the names of the Crew, because one of her cousins whose surname was Harris, a Flight Engineer was killed over Germany whilst flying with Bomber Command. I had only entered his initial on the form so told her his name was Johnnie and he came from Biggleswade in Bedfordshire, she was absolutely amazed when I also informed her my Engineer's Father was a policeman because her cousin's Father was also a policeman before retirement.

Anyhow, Johnnie our Engineer was her late cousin and as the family had never received details about how he was killed I was able to give her an account of the Nuremberg Operation and what happened to 'Q' Queenie and all the Crew, which she could pass on to the family, although Johnnie's parents had passed away many years before.

144

Otto, German Nightfighter pilot and myself at a reunion of Luftwaffe and RAF Aircrews at Largs, Germany Sept. 1998

To return to the visit to Germany in 1998, it ended when Jonathan drove me to Frankfurt Airport to catch the evening flight back to Manchester after which he and Jean would continue with their holiday in the Black Forest.

I was carrying the canvas bag containing lots of small pieces of 'Q' Queenie and on going through customs explained what they were and asked for permission to take them out of the Country. I shall never forget the looks on the faces of the German Customs Officers, one looked as though she thought me mad and the others with some amusement probably thought the same. However, after referring the matter to another colleague nothing was said so with a smile I went through thinking that it was the first time scrap metal had ever been declared.

So that was the end of my second visit to Germany to gain further information on my Lancaster 'Q' Queenie which is still giving up parts of itself after being buried in the ground for over fifty years. I wonder what the future will bring ? I know as long as Reiner Klug and his colleagues remain interested in the 'exhumation' many more parts will be detected and brought to the surface.

Renewing my partnership with Lancaster at East Kirby Heritage Centre and inviting Reiner into the Cockpit

Jonathan at the controls of the Lancaster at East Kirby with his "Flight Engineer"

I have already been advised of the possibility that a Merlin engine is buried in what was a bog in 1944 but the ground is now dry. The owner of the land at that time supplied this information and arrangements are to be made to obtain a special metal detector and permission to use it, hoping that the excavation proves successful.

Although the written part of my story is nearly complete I would never have thought when I joined the R.A.F. for aircrew duties in 1941 that in effect, fifty years later, my life would still be attached to that time by a Lancaster Bomber which was lost but is now making a reappearance and giving me back some parts of it which I still recognise.

It looks as though my story will be never ending because I can now add another find. Most of the small pieces from the wreckage are unidentifiable, but some are, and one of these, the blind flying instrument panel has recently been discovered. I must keep this as a reminder of times when I depended on the instruments to see us through some of the most atrocious flying conditions encountered in the winter of 1943/44.

Another find was handed to me on my second visit which adds a poignancy to the story, it is the Navigator's (Colin) Propelling Pencil which no doubt he was using when we were hit by the fighter. It is weather worn after lying in a wood for over fifty years but is still in working order.

Jonathan has done a marvellous job by mounting it on a polished wooden plaque, secured by clips on to a metal base. I have also placed it on the mantelpiece next to the brass detonator.

However, as a postscript to my story I have to refer to a most important meeting I had a few months ago with Carl, the Navigator / Radio Operator in Martin Becker's Me 110 Night Fighter.

It was at a reunion of Luftwaffe Night Fighter Crews and members of the Doncaster Air Gunners Association at Laage near Rostock to which I was invited, and Carl who had been informed of my visit knew I was interested in tactics used by Martin Becker when he shot down our Lancaster on the Nuremberg Raid.

The first point was to compare our records with those of the Luftwaffe for 30th/31st March 1944, to ascertain the position where we were shot down, and according to the log he had of British bombers destroyed the entry made for 'Q' Queenie was 12 miles North West of Wetzlar, a difference of 2 kilometres only from our calculations.

Although Carl could not especially remember the destruction of our aircraft ; Becker shot down eight aircraft that night, he said they generally used the same tactic when a bomber was visually identified. Most of what he then told me confirmed my impression of the attack and answered questions which I had on my mind.

I always thought a night fighter attack was made from port quarter down, i.e. on the left hand rear of the aircraft to fire upwards in to the

147

Jonathan-Walter Paris-Dick Starkey
Walters Apartment. London 1999

wing to hit the petrol tanks and engines and set the aircraft on fire, also to line up the cockpit to disable the pilot ; this action was carried out only if the gunners in the bomber had not seen the fighter and given the pilot a corkscrew evasive action.

Becker, however, used a different method ; if his aircraft had not been 'picked up' as he stalked the bomber, he approached it on the starboard rear side at a lower altitude, pulled up the nose of the aircraft and commenced a skidding movement from right to left by applying rudder, at the same time firing with all his armament into the bomber.

As I follow this description, Becker's attack on the Lancaster fits my impression of the way he destroyed 'Q' Queenie and killed two of my crew ; George Walker - Wireless Operator and Jock Jameson - Mid Upper Gunner.

One of the first parts of 'Q' Queenie given to me on our second visit to Germany was the piece of perspex from the cover of the H2s scanner situated underneath the aircraft, forward of the rear turret, which had a perfect 20mm shell hole through it. As the Rear Gunner was not hit (he acknowledged my order to bale out) it would appear the attack was made at a fairly steep angle which hit the perspex and came on at a slightly less angle, possibly because Becker had dipped the nose of his aircraft a little to hit the mid upper turret and Wireless Operator's position ; killing both lads, this could be the reason why they were the only two crew who did not acknowledge the order to bale out.

The Fighter then continued the skidding movement to port still firing with all he had, to hit the mainplane and port outer engine setting them on fire, and possibly hitting the inner engine ; the trajectory of the bullets and cannon then followed a course to pass the cockpit window about 18" from my head but some hitting the aircraft around my feet which caused the injury to my foot by flying shrapnel.

The fire in the mainplane and engine was so severe it reached the petrol tanks in approximately 15 seconds, when they exploded and blew the wing off.

In the few seconds between the Lancaster being set ablaze and exploding with all the bombs still aboard there was no further attack. I was told by Carl that this was because Becker never made a second attack if the first one produced a large fire in the engines and mainplane to render the aircraft incapable of staying in the air. Becker knew from experience when a bomber was 'going down'.

The meeting with Carl was so meaningful because I was able to fit the observations and records he produced into a picture of 'Q' Queenie's last moments which had remained unfinished in my mind for all those years.

Postscript

When I started writing this story, I knew I had to try and find our Bombaimer Wally Paris. Over the last few years I have been unsuccessful in my quest; but Jonathan recently received a telephone call from Claudio of the Herborn Air War Society in Germany, who had also been trying to establish his whereabouts, that the British Inland Revenue had agreed to forward a letter from him to Wally.

He thought it amusing that a foreigner should be the recipient of such a favour from the Inland Revenue when it was denied to a British Citizen. However he wrote to Wally giving him my address, and to my surprise after 55 years I received a letter from him.

I telephoned him at his home in London because I wanted to know how he was and what happened to him after he baled out of "Q" Queenie on the night of 30th/31st March 1944.

He told me he returned to his studies at Edinburgh University after the war and after graduating took a job in India, where he worked for 23 years before returning home and continuing with the same employment until retirement.

After recovering from the shock of hearing my voice he said he was in fairly good health and was married to an Indian lady.

He said he landed in a tree after escaping from the aircraft, and after extracting himself, walked away from the area, but was picked up by the Germans next day and transferred to Dulag Luft Interrogation Centre.

As he was the only one to bale out of the Lancaster I asked him if he saw it explode(at the time he did not know that there were still six of us in the aircraft). He saw the aircraft going down in a mass of flames but could not remember seeing it explode; however he recalled seeing a massive glow followed by what he thought was the sound of a single engined aircraft rapidly approaching him.

As he baled out at approximately 18,000 feet and fell probably 2000 feet before he opened his parachute, he would be short of oxygen and probably semi-concious when he saw the large glow, which could have been the aircraft exploding and what he thought was a single engined plane could have been one of the Merlin engines still running after being detached from the aircraft when it disintegrated. (The Germans had no single engine fighters operating that night, if there were any it would have been over the target area).

"Before finishing this last part of the story, I must refer to a broadcast made on BBC Radio Sheffield several months ago when I was invited to talk about the Nuremberg raid and the discovery of the remains of our Lancaster by Claudio's Air War Society at Herborn. During the broadcast I said that Wally was the only other survivor and efforts were being made to trace him.

It was absolutely marvellous when he was found and I informed Radio Sheffield of our success.

A further broadcast was arranged and Claudio in Germany and Wally in London agreed to take part by telephone link.

All through the story I have commented about the surprise and sometimes amazement at some of the findings; and the broadcast produced a further surprise when Wally referred to my order for the crew to bale out. He said Joe, the rear gunner, after acknowledging the order said the incendiaries had been ignited and set the fuselage on fire. I have always been of the opinion that he could not bale out because his turret which was powered by the port outer engine was put out of action when I feathered the engine to try and stop the fire spreading.

Since the attack I had struggled to try and control the aircraft and as a result must have missed his comments about the fire; and this, and not the feathered engine, could have been the reason for him saying he could not escape.

If a fire did break out in the fuselage it would have been well behind the cockpit, and as no response was made by George, the Wireless Operator or Jock the Mid Upper Gunner about the fire or baling out they must have been killed by the attack.

It was no wonder a fire in the fuselage, together with those in the port outer engine and wing, quickly spread until the aircraft exploded within such a short time and the ensuing fire ball fed by the 1600 gallons of high octane fuel would flash through the fuselage towards my unconscious body, with only a narrow cushion of air in front of it to protect me from being burnt to death; before I was hurled through the perspex cover, like a cork from a bottle, into the night sky"

I shall be contacting Wally again when I hope to make arrangements to meet him and we can have a talk about old times with the crew of the Squadron.

So the time has come to end my story so far and what has become increasingly incredible since I started it is the way all the people still alive, both the British and the German, who were involved in the activities both in the air and on the ground, on the night of 30th/31st March 1944 have since come together.